Tip from Jane:
Please refrain
from explaining
or complaining
that writing is a pain
and drives you insane.
Writing can be illuminating and fun,
especially when you are done!

–Pamela Kleibrink Thompson
inspired by Jane Freund's Pixie Chicks group

For more information, please contact

Freundship Press, LLC
PO Box 9171
Boise, ID 83707
(208) 407-7457
www.freundshippress.com
info@freundshippress.com

First printing 2011

ISBN 978-0-982204-5-0

To order additional copies of this book, contact Freundship Press as listed above.

Introduction
by Jane Freund

"If there's a book you really want to read, but it hasn't been written yet, then you must write it." -- Toni Morrison

Simply put, becoming a published author takes courage and I am proud of each and every woman in this book and the courage they demonstrated by being a part of this book. Sharing one's writing with others isn't as easy as it sounds but requires putting a piece of oneself out for public comment. As Walter Wellesley "Red" Smith said "There's nothing to writing. All you do is sit down at a typewriter and open a vein."

Since I have been writing professionally, I have had all sorts of people talk with me about becoming published writers. Some talk about writing and probably have more books on writing than they know what to do with, but probably do little if any actual writing. Others will write, but don't want to get published or don't know how and don't want to ask how as they don't believe that it's a possibility. Still others write and have the dream of being published, but don't know where to start. I have been all three of those types of writers in my life so I can relate.

In 2007, I left Boise State University and ten years of teaching Communication to pursue writing and publishing as a full-time career. But since the teaching and education bugs stayed with me, I developed and taught a workshop titled *Writing Until I Get it Right – How to be a Published Author.*

Two years ago, I was teaching this writing workshop and the participants were four women. As the discussion continued, we discovered that each of us had had pixie haircuts as young girls. As a result, the Pixie Chicks' Writers Group was born on Facebook. Consisting of over 200 women around the world, the members encourage one another in our various writing projects.

This book is a compilation of writings by over two dozen members of the Pixie Chicks' Writers Group. What is contained within these pages is as diverse as the women who wrote this material. You will find poetry, recipes, life essays, short stories and other forms of opening a vein.

Through my professional writing career, I have been blessed with two terrific mentors, Mary Ellen Arndorfer and Susan Stacy. They taught me a great deal about the ins and outs of the writing business and have helped me over the years as I have developed ideas and strategies for writing and publishing. However, I also learned a great deal through the proverbial school of hard knocks. In order to pay forward what Mary Ellen and Susan taught me and to help others negotiate the writing maze, I decided to create an opportunity for budding writers to become published authors. The result is this book which is truly an eclectic collection representing the variety of talents, backgrounds, and gifts of the woman who wrote it.

Speaking of which, thank you to the authors whose names are included both inside the pages and on the cover. Special thanks to Thom Hollis and Suzanne Ames for designing the book's cover, Gena Shikles for editing the content, and Caxton Printers of Caldwell, Idaho for printing the book.

Finally, this book is dedicated to budding writers, regardless of gender, who dream of getting their works published. If you think too many hurdles exist to getting published, let me close with a quote from Henry Ford: "Obstacles are those frightful things you see when you take your eyes off your goal."

Keep on writing!

Table of Contents

Poetry

Life Essays

God in My Life

Short Stories

Cooking Creativity

In Conclusion

Eclectic Poetry

A Day in September

by Suzanne McHone

The special effects are stupendous.
Buildings sift into their own bellies
like sandcastles.
Flight attendants realign their jargon:
Peanuts? Coffee? Would you like cremation
with that?
Film is spliced. The leader rallies
his mind. "Can we
have a moment of silence
for the screaming victims
of this crime?" Over coffee
I watch our nation's icons
delete. I wake my boy.
He listens for the recruiter's call.
I wish it was just a movie.

At Auction
by Buffy Naillon

The soft dirt
beneath my feet
gives no hint
of the coming thunder

Nobody notices it
over the auctioneer's voice
the hands of the men
flapping like birds desperate
to take flight

Nobody notices it
as they crowd
together like cattle in a train car
shoving popcorn
and candy
and Coors Light
into their mouths

Nobody notices the coming thunder
the dancing hooves
of a spirited auburn yearling
jumping and spitting
like water drops in a hot frying pan

And then the storm from within
ERUPTS
and cannot be contained
by any rope nor good intention

And the sound of thunder
escapes, escapes, escapes
the equine mouth
and electric lightning
runs free from young hooves

flashes of white hot high in the air
glisten against the dusk
in the arena

And with a flash of the magician's hand
a young horse
mesmerizes and calms
the storm and quiets the thunder
with only a few secret words
whispered
and the glimmering
of her corn husk hair
in the dying sun

And I can feel the storm
at last
in the soft dirt beneath my feet

At Auction 2

by Buffy Naillon

I stand in a stable
sun softly comes in
and makes fairy dust
of the loose, powdery dirt
beneath my feet
floating in on air

It sparkles, shimmers
all around me
enchanting the horse
who has become
my friend through the bars
as he tried gently
to kiss me
with velvet lips

And I know his tiny horse kisses
and soft breath
brushing gently on my cheek
are the only tastes of freedom
that either of us will get
standing there in the stable
separated by the steel bars between us

For soon
the auctioneer's call
will send him to
someone else's home
to become someone else's friend
and I'll drive home
alone in my car

By The Edge Of The Sea

by Sharon S. Brown

Layers of memories
Lap at the shoreline
Of my mind
Like sea foam lace
Swirling endlessly
Without measure
Leaving sandy traces
Of sentiment
In my heart
As I amble barefoot
Through salty waters
Of dried up tears
From ancient days
Of my prehistoric past
When I thought
Nothing else mattered
I could only see
That which lay
In the path
Before me
At that time
I did not have
The strength
To look up
I could not focus
My eyes to see
The dazzling vision
That beckoned
Up ahead
On the sublime horizon
Of my life

I meander through
Braids of seashells
And seaweed
At the water's edge

Of those bygone days
Of my past
And stop to pick up
Specimens that catch
My eye
Some broken and smashed
From the angry sea
Of memories
Others still whole
And impossibly perfect
Plucked from
Subdued tidepools
Where mermaids and
Fairies glide
Among verdigris ribbons
In my daydreams
And I place them
Carefully
In the beach bag
Of my recollections
To take back
To the cottage
By the sea
Of my consciousness
Where I can
Examine each one
More closely
With tenderness

I want to remember
And forget
Simultaneously
And feel wiser
For having the courage
To live
By the primordial edge
Of that billowy sea
Where I once swam
In whirlpools

And high tides
Oh yes, I remember
Swimming naked
At early dawn
And in evening's twilight
In those salty
Turquoise waters
Of my life

Death

by Jennifer Orvis

From the first painful breath and unsteady step you follow close behind.
And once the young brain learns of you, your concept weights the mind.

Young or old, one or many, no preference do you make.
No second thoughts impede your duty or keep you from your take.

The mother hopes the new-filled crib you'll pass by without delay
But without regret you steal her dreams before the break of day.

You await the doomed on the battlefield, then collect them from the ground.
Your burden then do you pass to angels soaring heaven bound.

It's not the bounty of summer's garden that you've come to reap.
It is the prize behind the eyes you give the Lord to keep.

Your arrival does all humanity fear and then abhor.
We can only hope that those we love don't wait upon your door.

Your omnipotence is undeniable and with it we must live.
But nothing calms the fear and dread that thoughts of you do give.

Elections
by Buffy Naillon

"I just want the country to be happy,"
said my husband one day
to no one in particular

"And I don't care if it takes
Ronald McDonald
being president to do it"

How would that be? Ronald McDonald as President?
Pictures of him with his golden arch halo
on every phone pole
on every street corner
in Everytown, USA?

Taking our money
in exchange for our votes

"Happy meals for the masses!"
he promises
only with better toys than the other guy
is offering
AND with the option of SUPERSIZING

Red perma-grin mouth speaking
Madison Avenue words
explaining why
his fast food policies
handed out at the drive
through window of convenience
are good for us

"Nutrition for the masses," he assures us

Milkshake, sugar-high euphoria
induces diabetic coma
causing him to forget to mention
that his freedom fries
give us all high cholesterol
and fat butts

Empty Nester

by Fran Finkbeiner

high above Staircase Rapids
the Tanager's nest is cozily cupped
in the horizontal fork of a weathered white pine
with ancient, knotted roots

empty
save for a few shards of
pale blue eggshells

she perches on a branch
high above the roaring water
watching her last fledgling
take flight

she waits
until his wings
fade into the hazy sunshine
and then begins to sing
a melody of sweet exultation
mixed with a few notes of sorrow

Engraved in Silver
by Sharon S. Brown

Don't know why I didn't see it
Coming my way
That silver bullet
With my name
Engraved upon it
Heading straight for my heart
Piercing me clear through
Shattering my trust
Sending pieces of me
Flying everywhere
With my mind reeling
From the pain

Don't know why
I didn't see it coming
Guess I was distracted
By the Love
I thought I saw
In your eyes
Well, I knew you carried a gun
And could hit your mark with ease
But I didn't know it was loaded
Never thought for one moment
That you would
Aim it right at me

And pull the trigger

July

by Judy Ferro

'Twas noon and brakes on bicycles
Did gripe and grumble in the heat.
All sticky were the handlebars
And sweaty was the rider.

"Beware July," the sun proclaimed,
"The fire that burns, the heat that withers!"
"July, July," the heat waves chimed,
"Our fine and fiery kiln--

Too hot for whirling spokes and hubs,
Too hot for pedals, chains and haste."
"Not so, not so," the tireless child
Shouted out with brimming joy.

Pedals whirred and wheels did spin
As rider soared on through the heat,
Until a breeze she did enlist
To battle proud July.

'Tis noon and brakes on bicycles
Do gripe and grumble in the heat.
All sticky are the handlebars,
But dauntless is the rider.

Junked Wurlitzer

by Suzanne McHone

Memorabilia gathers 'round—like we did
at the beer joint--
turning a deaf ear to your legacy.
You rest amidst rusted fenders,
winged roadsters, a Royal Crown Cola sign.
Junk once as luminous as you were.

You were a wooer of the juvenile
Calling us to dance; satisfying your voyeuristic soul.
Now you wear a tarp. Army green
like the uniforms that marched to your tune;
victorious in purpose.

Remember? You led Rex and Viv in the Foxtrot?
The night he bailed?
Mitch and Stella mastered the Charleston
to your tricky syncopation.

B 3 brought our feet to the floor.
T 57 kept them there.
D 19 drew our bellies close.
J 32 kept them that way.
Harbinger of bliss, commissioner of fate;
sending the innocent into battle,
the old back into adolescence.
Conniver of reality,
contractor of dreams;
know your duty is done.

Ode to a Rose

by Sharon S. Brown

O Beauteous Rose
How I wonder
You spring forth
Though torn asunder
Your fragrance fills
The air divine
As I capsize
With Love
The pleasure's mine
To hold so close
To hold so dear

O Beauteous Rose
Do you hear
The nightbird calling
Singing, trilling
Ever longing
For the warmth
Of his embrace
Though he departed
Without a trace

O Beauteous Rose
Do tell me how
You still bloom
Even though
Your every treasure
Was plucked from you
With a great pleasure
Your petals fallen
One by one
Till you are left
With not a one
But for a thorny throat
O Beauteous Rose

Paint Chip #13

by Fran Finkbeiner

midnight mares
gallop through
darkened dreams
chasing me
taunting me
until I realize
that even in slumber
I have poetic license
to change
demon horses
into water colored ponies
and choose the one
with tie-dyed tail
to ride into morning

Paint Chip # 18
by Fran Finkbeiner

in my Flying M coffee
the color of *honey sand*
floats an O'Keefe flower
too beautiful to sip

Red Bouquet

by Sharon S. Brown

Abundant bouquet
Of blushing red
Gladiolas
Overflowing
With elegance
From your powerful arms
Like graceful ballerinas
Gathered together
Draped in crimson gowns
And wearing tiaras
Adorned
With dewdrops
Their long necks
Extended
In supple poses

You bought them
For me
In a spontaneous
Moment
A romantic gesture
That delightful evening
Last summer
As warm breezes
Softly teased
The ambient mood
When you told me
I looked
~ Delicious ~
It had been
A month
Since we last saw
Each other
And we were
Hungry

Flowers offered
With such tenderness
In strong
Yet gentle hands
That could have easily
Crushed
Those delicate blossoms
You were
So courtly
When you handed
That wildly
Gorgeous bouquet
To me
As if you were
Prince Charming
Presenting me
With an enchanted
Glass slipper
I felt
Like a princess
Yes
Even at my age

Later
Standing at
My kitchen sink
In blue jeans
You took time
To trim the ends
And casually
Arrange
Long emerald stems
With scarlet blooms
In a crystal vase
Especially for
~ Me ~

And it was
Then
In that moment
As you stood
There
Arranging that bouquet
When my heart
First took notice of
~ You ~
And flew away
Soaring
To uncharted realms
I knew not where
Like unfurling petals
Plucking
My resolve
To remain
Elusive

It was in
That moment
When you stole
~ My heart ~
You and
Your red bouquet

Roadtrip Lessons, Part One

by Fran Finkbeiner

Cornstalks saluted me.
Head stuck out the window.
Sucking in Indiana
exorcising
from my lungs
the demons blown there
from four varicose veined,
cross bearing,
chain smoking
women.
They took turns
back seat driving,
one-handed puppeteers
pulling the driver's string.
Me, audience of one,
melted to my vinyl seat
Silky strands of conversation
spun a delicate web
of soap-opera strength
through the smoky haze.
They prattled on about
the neighbors' failing marriage,
whispered about
that girl with child,
and whether the new Priest
truly believed in Purgatory.
Discussions ebbed
to soft silence somewhere
near Missouri.
Gossip Goddesses, Grandmothers all,
they taught me the important things:
How to chase fireflies in the dark of night
How to recognize the male cardinal
it's glory crowned in a blaze of red.

Stars in My Eyes

by Sharon S. Brown

I went walking in the moonlight
Down a darkened path
Feeling my way into the night
Like a maiden tiptoeing into her bath

The full moon floated above me
Guiding me all the way
Until I came upon a twinkling sea
Of starlight that beckoned me to play

So I frolicked in the Milky Way
As reflected on the ground
Until I stood before a ray
Of Light so incredibly profound

As I stepped into the spotlight
Something swirled around me
'Twas the velvet curtains of the night
Parting to reveal her dark beauty

I peered into the vastness of the night
And saw You standing there
A radiant heavenly body shining bright
With moonbeams in your hair

I stood back and considered you from afar
For I was dazzled by the view
You wore a sparkling crown of stars
And flashed those eyes of blue

Oh, the sight of your handsome pose
Caught me by surprise, my breath too
As Cupid's swarm of arrows
Pierced me through and through

I tried to run, wanted to hide
But found I could not move
And even though indeed I tried
I stood frozen there, not knowing what to do

With one hand holding onto a stream
Of the shimmering Aurora Borealis
You reached out your other hand to me
And transformed me into an enchanted Goddess

I closed my eyes, and lost myself in the sweetness
Of your southern charm, a seductive Eden
The sapphire sky whirled all about us
As the attraction began to deepen

You unraveled the satin ribbons on
The gossamer gown that I was wearing
And as it fell upon the lawn
My shy heart reveled in the sharing

Then you wrapped me up in a veil of stars
And drew me into your warm embrace
That's when I knew the night was ours
To see the glow of Love reflected in your face

We began to dance and sway as one
As you played me softly like a flute
I drank freely of your sweet love potion
And hungered for the taste of your forbidden fruit

Together we waltzed across the universe
To a distant galaxy, another side of heaven
You romanced me with such amorous verse
As star-crossed lovers we seemed destined

Truly you cast a spell on me, My Love
One not easily broken, so charmed I was by you
It seemed we fit together like hand in glove
I believed every word you spoke was true

And when Dawn came to whisper my name
Leaving a kiss of dew upon my face
I awoke from the reverie of Passion's flame
To find you had vanished without a trace

I looked towards the morning sky
Searched through the azure skies of blue
Were you just a shooting star who caught my eye
Was I only dreaming of a love so rare and true

Although from my life you did depart
I loved every moment I spent with you
My Love, I still carry you around in my heart
And these stars remind me of You

The Bandicoot Pack
by Suzanne McHone

Way down under where the wallabies roam,
a pack of bandicoots make their home.

When they're not out sneaking through joints and halls,
crashing soirees or slipping through malls,

They settle back in their hollow abode
to plan the next time they'll hit the road.

Honcho, Dag, Peter and Sam,
thieving bandits that pillage the land.

It's not gold or silver their hearts desire.
Money and treasures do not inspire.

But guitars and banjos, don't ever loan them!
They'll steal your songs and sing 'em like they own 'em.

New York City, their next destination.
The Broadway stage, their target location.

They hit the dressing rooms at a quarter of four,
try every costume and hunger for more.

Just before curtain, the stars come along
but those crazy bandicoots stole every song.

Up comes the curtain with all in their places.
Oh, the looks on the audience's faces.

No sound comes out. Not even a toot.
The bandicoots run for the door with the loot.

The constable says, "Boys, you're way out of order,
packing those songs straight for the border."

Then with a growl, a grunt and a snort,
he hauled them all off to his kangaroo court.

With plenty of time to ponder their fault,
the songs locked tight in the evidence vault,

Their criminal ways should have been mended
but as you might guess, that's not where it ended.

Under cover of night, they broke away quick.
Like a band of brothers, those four were thick.

Back to the core of the Coolabah tree
to plan the next time they'd set out on a spree.

The Butterfly

by Sharon S. Brown

I remember her
When she resided
For a season
In the garden of my life

With wings of gold
Dipped in blue
A Butterfly
As fresh as dew

Freed at last
From her cocoon
Ripe for her debut

With trembling wings
She took flight
Leaving silky shadows
In the light

Across the lawn
She danced and floated
Quivering like a ballerina
On opening night

As the curtain parted
I saw her there
Gliding on a moonbeam
With rose petals in her hair

On she flew
Fluttering about
O, where did she go?
Look, over there . . .

Splashing in a fairy's pool
Shivering with delight
Till drops of water
Like strings of pearl
Slipped from her velvet wings
An ethereal sight

Too soon, I knew
This Butterfly
Would yearn to see
What lies beyond
The garden wall
For the garden
Could not contain her

And the day did come
When off she flew
Into the wide horizon

While I remain here
To bloom again
For yet another season

I cannot follow
I have no wings
The most that I can do
Is toss my seeds
Into the breeze
And hope they land
Somewhere

For I am a Flower
In this garden of Life
A Flower
Who has seen
The maiden dance
Of a Butterfly
From a front row seat

The Purchase
by Suzanne Ames

In loving memory of my father: Everett J. (Bing) Ames

Walking through the door of the local liquor store,
she hoped her purchase would bring her some peace
Watching her father die had left emptiness inside,
a hole in her heart she hoped to fill with peace.

She stood looking at the bottles, all lined up on the shelves.
She wondered which one, if any, would help.
When suddenly she heard him, his voice so loud and clear.
She quickly looked around to see if anyone else could hear.

This is not the answer and you know it in your heart.
The answer is for you to see, we will never be apart.
She felt his arms around her, as he whispered in her ear.
Please do not define me by the hours of my death,
but by the way I lived, with honesty and no regrets.

She knew then that he was with her and all would be okay.
He would walk beside her proudly each and everyday.
She turned and walked toward the door of the local liquor store.
She didn't make her purchase, she didn't need to anymore

The Ritual

by Judy Ferro

We've ousted an incumbent!
Hooray! Hoorent!
Our lives were a mess,
Full of crime, grime and duress--
All 'cause of that preda-political gent.

We've elected a president!
Hooray! Hoorent!
He oozes pizzaz,
With toothy saxy-matazz,
Our smiling and guiling and styling a-gent.

We've discovered a Lancelot!
Hooray! Hoo--what?
It's been six minutes,
Twice a boiled egg limit--
What's stalling our healthy and wealthy Camelot?

We're stuck with an incumfail!
Oh woe! Oh wail!
The country's amuddle,
Mired in tax-lax befuddle,
Blame that elective, defective scape-a-male!

The Sands of Time
by Sharon S. Brown

You ask about my fame and fortune
Throughout the entirety of my life
Did I have too much or too little
Or has it been just right

What fame and what fortune
And who cares anyway
My worth is far greater
Than the contents of my resume

With only my bare footprints
I hope to leave this life
Footprints indelibly etched
Upon the eternal sands of time

Footprints left by the depth
Of my inner qualities
Within my heart and soul
And some measure of humility
Not borne from the weight
Of my external accessories

My footprints will not be
Well-heeled, certainly not refined
Mine will be calloused and worn
That's how my life has been defined

For I have walked anonymously
Upon my path through this life
And I have known the richness of
Life's struggle and the strife

But I shall leave behind priceless treasures
When my time comes to depart
My grandson's eyes, my granddaughter's smile
These are my legacy, bequeathed from my heart

Today I Set My Spirit Free
by Sharon S. Brown

Today I set my spirit free ~

Let go of the past
That still haunted me
Released the pain
That clung so tightly

Forgave unkind words
That had been spoken
Forgot about promises
That have been broken

Put down the sword
That I'd been carrying
Laid down that hatchet
That needed burying

Handed over burdens
That weighed me down
And all those worries
Which made me frown

Cast off doubts
That held me back
Stopped keeping score
No need to keep track

Held my tongue
Tempered my comments
Dropped preconceived notions
That clouded my judgment

Freed myself from the fear
That held me in chains
Stepped into sunshine
And out of the rain

Yes, today I set my spirit free ~

Opened up my heart
Embraced my vulnerability
Examined my motives
And took responsibility

Looked for God
In every face
Within human frailty
I saw Grace

And saw the Beauty ~

In every moment
Of every day
Life seems far richer
When lived that way

Rebuilt bridges
Mended fences
Extended many
Olive branches

Reached out my hand
To those in need
Sowed compassion
Planted seeds

Forgot about myself
For awhile
Took a stroll
Wore a smile

Stopped along the way
To smell the roses
Forgot about time
Enjoyed the moment

Turned a corner
Within my soul
Relinquished control
Went with the flow

Much more content
To let things be
And enjoy the peace
Of tranquility

Savor time spent
In a contemplative mood
Reflecting on life
In my solitude

Learning to walk
In humility
And transcend my ego
For all eternity

Did I finally remove
That weight on my shoulder
Or perhaps this is the wisdom
That comes with getting older

Today I set my spirit free ~

I stood in the Light
And let It wash over me
And became the Lighthouse
My soul was always meant to be

By accepting the Red Rose
Of Love into my heart
I Thank You, Great Spirit
For this brand new start

True Confession
by Sharon S. Brown

I am having a secret love affair
It is always on my mind
I dream about a lover's tryst
Morning, noon, and night

I don't mean to ignore you
Or betray you in any way
Yet I carry my secret love affair
Around in my heart and mind all day

Who is this secret lover, you wonder
Who competes for my affections with you
Perhaps now is the time to confess
That I'm in love with creative writing too

I love to spend forbidden time with my new flame
Love to sneak away every chance I get
As inspired words and phrases formulate in my mind
At my keyboard, I am a love slave to my manuscript

I know at times you think me absent-minded
My attention seems to wander
I may not devote all my time to you
For in my imagination do I saunter

Please don't take it personally
Don't get your feelings hurt
No need to feel jealous
Of my love affair with words

For I pour out my heart and soul
Onto the printed page
I'm not saying that my phrasing is any good
Or that my words are profound or sage

But I have the soul of an artist
And this web page is my canvas
I splash words and phrases around like paint
The process leaves me breathless

There now, I've confessed it
My secret is known to all
I'm having a secret love affair
With the musings that I scrawl

You see, I have the soul of an artist
Deep within me the passion does burn
I can no longer deny it
To my work-in-progress, I must return

You may think me fickle
And that I am a shameless coquette
You may wonder if I have a roving eye
And regret the day we met

Please don't hold this against me
Instead let me embrace
My passion for writing poetry
Before these words vanish without a trace

And in the process I will immortalize
My love for you as well
Did you know that YOU are my muse
And that over me you have cast a spell

For it is YOU whom I long to write about
I compose my rhapsodic verse especially for you
Though I may take poetic license here and there
Every nuance comes straight from my heart, this I swear is true

(Untitled)

by Fran Finkbeiner

For days, I've nurtured
this bundle of meter and metaphor
rejoiced in its first iambic beats
its first hazy draft, tiny discernible form

I can feel it's none too subtle kick
telling me there's little comfort
in the confines of my mind
The gestation period is near its end

Dilation of thought and need
bring forth rhythmic contractions
words woven by the maker's hands
propelled along the birth canal
nudged from its protective
cocoon of anonymity

With a deep breath
I bear down
One
two
thr
ee
pu
sh
e
s

and she is
birthed
into print

(Untitled)
by Fran Finkbeiner

In that space
between
darkness and dawn
birds begin
their sunrise symphony
sweet songs
stir me from slumber

(Untitled)

by Fran Finkbeiner

I
spill myself
across
blank canvas
immediately
soaked up, spread out
separated
from
who I thought
I was

Where My Love Blooms

by Sharon S. Brown

Oh My Love, what I wouldn't give
To be a flower in the garden where you live
As my silken petals reach out to touch your face
My leafy tendrils, like fingers, would softly trace
Your cheek, your brow, your tender lips
Curling down to caress your waiting fingertips
All the exquisite parts of you that I long to kiss
Sun-drenched days could never give me such enchanted bliss

And if you would grant me one heavenly pleasure
As you move in closer, let me savor
The sweetness of your breath as you lean my way
To smell the fragrance of my delicate bouquet
And if you lingered near me, I would sigh
If I were but a flower in the garden of your life

For wherever resplendent flowers bloom
So does my deepest love for you
May you savor Love's sweetest perfume
Through morning, noon, and nighttime too
... and *Remember Me Always*

Why do You Ask?

by Judy Ferro

Do I have a leprechaun?
Well…no, not a one.
Though once I had three—
Somber George,
dull, dull John,
and Lloyd Eustace.

Lloyd Eustace? That was a pen name.
He kept a printing press
In my left shoe—
Oh, the tales
I made up
to go barefoot!

No, three wasn't too many.
A wide collar could hide three or four,
Maybe even more--
It's different today…
No collars and
No leprechauns.

Now, why won't you let me cut your hair?

With Pen In Hand

by Sharon S. Brown

Poetic wanderings of the mortal mind
Sprung from the heart and soul
Leaving inky footprints throughout time
Searching for an immortal home

Evocative words scrawled on a page
Struggling for rhythm and rhyme
On and on cramped fingers race
Composing line upon line

Yet still the finish line eludes
The poem striving to run free
Streams of words describe complex moods
Still, the composition lacks profundity

Until one day Love came along
To find tender phrases dawning
And Love's infusion created Song
With melodic notes of human longing

WRITER'S NOTE: I wrote this poem for my darling daughter, Shari Alana, on her 27th birthday. She had been grown and gone for several years and I was living in Ft. Lauderdale at the time, she in Seattle, with a million miles between us. Not much has changed in the ensuing years, for as life would have it, we have traded coastlines, and there are still a million miles between us, yet no distance separates our hearts.

Admittedly, this poem may be too syrupy for some, but the sentiment comes from a mother's heart, to which I think most parents can relate, including fathers, particularly if you were blessed with a lovely daughter as I was/am.

Life Essays

A Ride on the Student Special

by Martha Kuhn

On a beautiful September day in 1945, a group of young men and women from Idaho Falls boarded the "Idaho Special" at the Pocatello train depot. As I remember, there were eight women and four men with me and a number boarding from the Pocatello area.

World War II had ended less than a month before. Even though the war had not affected us directly, we were much aware during our four years of high school that a horrible event was occurring. Yet we did not really suffer, except when our mothers ran out of sugar before a ration stamp was valid. Or when we could not take the family car because there were no more gas stamps or could not have a new pair of shoes because they were also rationed. *Then* we were very aware.

We all knew some young men who had left for the service. But in eastern Idaho, we did not feel the war directly. Probably the worst was when even the girls had to thin sugar beets and pick potatoes because there were not enough young men to do the work.

Now here we are, off on the biggest adventure of our lives: college. The Pocatello station was filled with parents and departing students and soon there were tearful good-byes as we boarded one of the several cars reserved for prospective University of Idaho students.

With the war over the government was trying to get the troops home,and they deserved the best rail cars. The ones we were in were ancient. There was a "pot bellied" stove at one end of the car I was in. The restrooms were primitive and, of course, seats were for both sitting and sleeping. No such thing as a sleeping car for us.

It was exciting when we approached Boise, we could see the Capitol building and the beautiful train depot. The areas around the depot were swarming with students and their families. Some of us felt a bit intimidated by the Boise girls and we thought they were very sophisticated. However, within a week, I found myself living in the Gamma Phi Beta sorority house with eight of those Boise girls and found we were much the same.

How were we dressed? First, you must remember that the train engine was coal-fired so everything was covered with a layer of soot. No matter. We *had* to be appropriately dressed: suits, hats, high heels and gloves. I wore an avocado green suit with skirt (no such things as pantsuits then) with matching blouse, a brown hat with up-turned brim and brown high heels. This was long before panty hose, so our stockings were silk (all the nylon went to make parachutes) and held in place by either a garter belt or girdle. There were all those well-dressed young ladies in a old dirty train car heading out of Boise.

I have no recollection of eating, as I am sure we did not have access to the dining car. One of my friends, Dorothy Rankin Johansen, remembers that five of the Boise girls had lunches packed by their mothers in hatboxes. Phyllis Halley Tapper said she seemed to remember getting off the train (maybe in La Grande, Oregon) and crossing over the tracks to eat in a hotel.

Our coaches were attached to the Portland Rose, out of Salt Lake City, and headed to Portland. My friend, Patricia Bennett, missed the train when it went through Nampa. Her mother drove like mad in her grandfather's old Buick coupe to get her to Huntington, Oregon to catch our train.

During the night, Francis Adams Spofford said she was trying to find the bathroom and somehow got into the main train's dining car, only to discover the porters and waiters all asleep on the tables.

We were told our cars would be unhooked from the Portland Rose somewhere in Oregon and attached to another train. As night came on, it got cold; our pot bellied stove was not working. We got into our suitcases and dug out slacks to pull on under our skirts. How did we sleep? I don't remember, but I do remember sometime in the wee hours feeling and hearing the train being jerked back and forth and attached to the "milk train" that pulled us into Moscow.

It was twenty-four hours from the time we left Pocatello until we pulled into the Moscow depot. Fortunately, there were trucks to take our luggage, carefully tagged with our names and the name of the dorm we would be staying in during "rush week".

ja We must have been a sight, struggling off the train, clothes rumpled, in need of a bath, but with our hats firmly in place and with our gloves in hand (hopefully still white). We headed up to the University. We trudged (in our heels) past the Student Union Building and past the ATO house (where we got some whistles) then up the hill and finally, feet aching, we arrived at Hays Hall.

I rode the student special twice more after that first trip. But it was this first time I remember best. It was the beginning of a wonderful four years at the University of Idaho. Years that helped educate me and bring me friends I have had all these years. . . if only we'd had cameras.

Career Coach: Be Thankful For Your Uniqueness
by Pamela Kleibrink Thompson

During the filming of Some Like it Hot, actor Tony Curtis pointed out to director Billy Wilder that he was doing an impression of Cary Grant. Billy Wilder replied, "If I wanted Cary Grant, I would have hired Cary Grant."

There is no one else in the world exactly like you. You have talents, experiences, and a perspective that make you unique. Be grateful for your unique gifts. Nurture and develop them and utilize your strengths to add your unique vision and insights to the world. Your uniqueness is your most marketable quality. Yet many creative people make the mistake of chasing the latest fad or imitating the newest style.

It's tempting to chase trends or emulate successful people. I fell into this trap. Years ago I worked on a screenplay with a friend of mine I had known since high school. We were three quarters of the way done with our script and we decided to celebrate and went to the movies. We were enthralled with the escapades of Indiana Jones in the Raiders of the Lost Ark. We decided to rewrite our detective screenplay in the Indiana Jones style. We never finished it.

"I don't know the key to success, but the key to failure is trying to please everybody."-- Bill Cosby

Don't try to chase the market or try to please everyone. Imagine Leonardo da Vinci painting the Mona Lisa in a storefront window. People pass by giving him feedback on his work in progress. "I think her dress should be a lighter color." "Her smile should be bigger." "The painting should be bigger." "She should wear her hair up." "The background should be the city, not the mountains." "There is too much shadow under her chin." Can you imagine Leonardo changing the painting as people made comments, concerned about whether everyone would like La Gioconda when it was finished?

Those who allow their unique strengths to set them apart from the crowd are those who achieve milestones in science, art, and literature.

Whenever you are tempted to blend in and try to be popular with everyone, remind yourself of your uniqueness - your passion and goals. Dare to be different and you will achieve success. You can't be all things to all people. Rita Mae Brown reminds us: "The reward for conformity is that everyone likes you except yourself."

Be thankful that you are different from everyone else in the world. You have a unique contribution to make. Go ahead. Be distinctive. Originals are rare.

Designing Your Relationship With Your Designer

by RoChel Burtenshaw

There you sit at your kitchen table with countless stacks of paint samples for you to consider using to redo various rooms of your home. Many very helpful friends who know just enough to be dangerous have made recommendations about the new look your home should have. The problem is that most of them have not redone their homes this century let alone since the Brady Bunch first came on television. You don't want to be rude but then again, you don't want to be stuck with something you don't want to look at for the next decade or so. Then the thought hits you: maybe I should hire a design professional instead of tackling this process by myself. Let's look at some things to consider in hiring a design professional.

First of all, hiring a designer does NOT mean that you have no taste. A person who has taste knows that hiring the right designer to assist with decisions can produce a beautiful end result. The end result can be one attempt at the color of paint instead of 17 attempts to get the right color. One of my favorite clients painted her southern kitchen wall 17 times to find the right color of paint. She brought me in to help with her basement remodel because she had no energy left to forge forth into the paint store and start through the corn maze of paint colors the store had to offer (let alone start the intricate decision process of which shade of red to choose). Here was a lady who had nice taste but needed to hire the person that could make a paint deck seem more like it had five shades of red instead of 64 shades of red.

The next consideration is that a good designer will feel like a great fitting pair of shoes. The most important thing you should consider about your choice for a good designer is how you feel working with them. Are you comfortable in this person's presence? Would you feel relaxed while shopping for towels & sheets with them? You want to have a level of trust. This is a person who will eventually know what side of the bed you wake up on and more than likely more information about your personal life than you could ever begin to imagine. If this person is good, you'll be comfortable knowing that they know all they know about you. You need to have full confidence that they practice confidentiality with your every word just like the attorney does with his or her client.

You want to evaluate how much help you really want. Would you like to do some of the research, shopping, or painting yourself? Knowing how much help you are wanting from this person is a strong indication of how much your personalities need to flow. Again, you want to know this is someone you're comfortable with being privy to your family information. She will know things like where you keep the safe to how much space your underclothing take up. This person eventually fits in like a family member.

The next strategy is to get names of more than one designer and interview each of them to select the best fit. Ask professionals such as builders, contractors, and others who would know good design professionals. During the interview find out about how the designer would approach your project, his or her philosophy of design, and their pricing structure. Your interior designer needs to be just that, your interior designer. No one needs a designer who is creating their vision in your home or using your home as a guinea pig experiment. Get a sense of the repertoire you have with this person. You will be paying for this service and need that comfortable feeling mentioned earlier.

What you're really going to want is someone who has done versatile work and creates and helps facilitate your vision. When you have trust and are comfortable enough with this person's ability to get inside your mind's eye and create your vision, you have found your winning combination.

Finally, finding the right designer may take a little looking, but it is well worth the effort. Whether you struggle with the concern of the expense or the fear of losing the control of your project, building a home with a design professional can take immense stress out of the project. A good designer can save you time and money. For example, he or she will have vendors and sources and can help you with knowing where to best spend your budget.

Remember, a good designer can make your project fun and exciting. So instead of resisting a consultant, forge forward knowing you can find the right fit with an interior design professional.

Fit or Flat: Getting Your Novel in Shape

by Kathy McIntosh

Just like the people who pen them, novels in progress (and some in print) are subject to several physical ailments: flabbiness, sagging middles, lack of tension and tone, and just plain old flatness, no zip. As we do for our bodies, certain practices or exercises will help get them into shape. But beware. While walking the dog can help tone you, what Margie Lawson terms "walking the dog" in your novel can lead to flabbiness and bored readers.

When you include every detail of your protagonist's life, from the alarm's pealing to the kind of shower gel he uses to the cracking of two free range eggs into a cast iron skillet, you're walking the dog. TMI or too much information. And then…and then…and then….sounds like the report of an excited kindergartner, who assumes the listener wants to hear every moment of the day. Details are effective ONLY when they provide useful insights into your character's personality or the problem he or she faces. Details mean more when they are specific and have meaning to your character. Possibly some of the facts in that first sentence told you something about the character, but I would only include it if, say, I wanted my reader to know my protagonist uses iron skillets because he's deathly afraid of using aluminum.

Telling details, as they're often called, tell us something about the character or the scene. Showing the character cutting her food into tiny pieces and moving it around on the plate instead of consuming it provides more insight than her hair color, body type, and facial characteristics.

In your descriptions, include details that are important to your Point of View characters, details that evoke their emotions. Don't just catalog the scenery because you like your setting. Make it count for your characters and it will compel your readers to keep reading.

What about sagging middles? Pilates works at strengthening the body's core, creating a taut, attractive, strong middle. That's what we want in our writing too. One way to create that taut core in a novel is to strengthen the connecting tissue by applying tension and conflict. That strong line of tension and story question pulls you through to the end. Throughout the story arc, your protagonist must face a series of obstacles. Things must get worse, then worse yet. Oh, and even worse, before she uses her wits and talent to resolve those problems. But each chapter, each scene, also needs tension. An argument between the main characters isn't necessarily conflict or at least not compelling, page-turning tension.

In each scene the focal character wants something. You can create tension by making it hard to achieve that objective by putting up obstacles **and** by showing the emotions created in your Point of View (POV) characters as they struggle to achieve their objectives. Even better? Show the emotions created in the non POV character in the scene as observed by the POV character.

Pacing creates tension. Taut, rapid fire dialog without tags and with lots of white space on the page moves the scene along. Contrast that pace by using telling details to stretch a physical act beyond what you'd normally expect or by allowing your character a moment for reflection. A moment. A brief moment. Too much internal thought drains tension.

You want to make sure your protagonist is not getting what he or she wants from the scene. Nor is the reader. And that creates tension. And tension is like a girdle for a sagging middle.

Another cause of the sagging middle is including too much back story. We've learned that you need to delay back story until after the first 50 pages. That's a good lesson. It doesn't give you permission to dump back story, like a four cheese lasagna, into your middle. It will sag. Sprinkle the bits of essential back story throughout the middle and avoid the back story bulge.

Make things difficult for your protagonist, season lightly with the right details, show the emotion that each obstacle, each event, creates in your characters, and don't drown your reader in back story. You'll avoid flabbiness and achieve a tasty, toned tale.

Life Eternal

by Sheila DC Robertson

I'm trying to find the Pacific Ocean. I can hear its low, soothing rumble, but right now an Indian casino blocks my view. It is Sunday and the casino parking lots are jammed with cars. The billboard is telling me that The Fab Four are coming to pay tribute to the Beatles tonight. Another four blocks and I catch a glimpse of the surf between a carwash and a Jiffy Lube. I nose my car into a little lane overarched with old growth cedar and find myself wedged too close to someone's driveway with no way to turn around. A big sign in their yard says, "Obama's Middle Name is Hussein". I put the car in reverse.

Back out on the street I inch along looking for some public access to a beach I know is there. As a teen I could step out of my car and onto the wild stretches of sea grass and sand that was this beach fifty years ago. Then, its long expanse was usually empty except for an occasional surf fisher and a few beachcombers.

Three miles later I wonder how I have dragged the same scenes of mega-condos, drive thru coffee huts, and super sized motels all the distance from Boise. At last I spot a small sign between high fenced beach mansionettes that reads "To the Beach".

I drop over the fore dune into crowds of families and kite fliers, dogs, and Frisbee throwers all claiming patches of sand. Surfers cut the wave lines. Couples are snuggled down in the driftwood. A youth group is playing beach volleyball. Christian Rock blares from a boom box. Their sweatshirts read "Power, Glory, and Eternal Life".

After an hour everyone is far behind and my prints are the only ones along the waterline. I follow sea-ground shell shards forming white striations in the black magnetite sand. The sun is low and I head to the dunes to look for shell middens; signs that the area was used by early Native Americans who dumped oyster, clam, and mussel shells, fish bones and other refuse in piles. They lived in cedar longhouses and traded and slaved up and down the coast. Until the white missionaries stopped them, they celebrated their rank and status with elaborate potlatches that proclaimed their wealth. Decimated by white man's disease, their remnants were driven onto reservations and until the casino went in, they were ghost peoples confined to shreds of poor land. This coast was all theirs, possessed by their story. They left only the garbage piles like the one I am sitting on and a thin echo of their language in the names of rivers and forests that surround me: Siuslaw, Siletz, Alsea, Yachats. A language that is now dead, even to them.

As I watch the sun sink, I wonder if the next middens will be filled with latte lids and Happy Meal toys. Just beyond the littoral where storm-muscled rollers break on basalt, brown pelicans fish inch above the heaving water. Long, primary feathers skim the cresting waves as they feed their way north. The prehistoric lava, the primordial sea, and the primal migrational flight of fishing birds have long been the language of the coastline. Here it is the surety of lava and sea and annual migrations that define what is eternal.

Social Psychology

by Angie Lewis

Social psychology is defined by Fiske (2004) as, "the scientific attempt to understand and explain how the thoughts, feelings, and behaviors of individuals are influenced by the actual, imagined, or implied presence of other human beings." While an all-encompassing definition is necessary to get a quick grasp on the subject, it is important to know that social psychology is much more complex. Social psychologists study how other people influence our thoughts, feelings, and actions. Because almost everything people do is social, the subject itself is large and has many variables. Because of the enormity of the subject, it is more easily understandable if broken into the concepts listed above.

This special area of psychology is unique on its own and similar to sociology, but being more focused on the individual. While this area does study groups, it focuses more on how the presence of the group affects the individual, not the group as a whole. The remaining paragraphs will explain social psychology further by analyzing its four key characteristics, explaining situationism and its significance, and identifying and explaining five core social motives.

Four characteristics exist that are specific to the study of social psychology. One basic characteristic is that people are influenced by other people's presence. They do something that they would not have done otherwise without this presence. For example if a person were to dine alone versus with a group of people, that person would probably not take as much care in setting the table unless they had others to share the tradition.

Another characteristic is that human presence influences the individual whether it's actual, imagined, or implied. This statement demonstrates that humans do not need to be present to affect another person. In fact even their implied or imagined presence (a worn path or the thought of a reaction to one's own action) can affect a thought, feeling, or behavior of another individual.

A third characteristic is that human presence, whether it's actual, imagined, or implied, affects a person's thoughts and feelings. This interaction, whether real or otherwise, has an impact on the way a person thinks and feels about a situation. For example, a person comes across a lost child. This interaction may cause an individual to either help the child (a favorable social reaction) or to go about their business because they are afraid to be late for a meeting. This perception and reaction to the presence of another being leads to the final characteristic.

Lastly, these thoughts and feelings are relayed into a person's actions or behaviors. Basically a person interacts somehow with his or her environment and then this interaction has some influence on how the person thinks and/or feels. Through this cognitive process, a person will react in one way or another to this interaction through this series of events. This series of events is what characterizes social psychology as a unique subfield of psychology as a whole.

As evidenced above, Fiske gives an exceptional definition of social psychology. However to really understand this area of psychology, it is necessary to know and understand the five core social motives. Also according to Fiske, "We are motivated to get along with other people because it is adaptive to do so." Motives are something that drives a person's behaviors and the behavior in this situation is social interaction. Five of these motives have been determined and they are: to belong, to be understood, to enhance oneself, to trust, and to control.

The idea behind belonging is that that people need strong and stable relationships with other people. Belonging is a term that shares concepts with the other four motives and according to Fiske, "belonging to a group helps individuals to survive psychologically and physically" in every situation. Belonging not only benefits the individual, but also the group.

The motive, self-enhancing, can be used for two things. Self-enhancing is a motive to either maintain a person's own self-esteem or for the possibility of self-improvement. Again this motive is not only beneficial to the individual, but also to the group. When a person feels positive about themselves, they feel motivated to interact and participate within the group.

Another motive, understanding, is also significant. The understanding motive, called one of the most fundamental motives, demonstrates that people want to understand their environments and they want others to understand them. An understanding can help an individual, as well as a group, adapt to the unexpected.

Trusting is also a motive for individuals to interact in social settings. According to Boon, trust involves "confidence or faith that some other, upon whom we must depend, will not act in ways that occasion us painful consequences" (Fiske, 2004). Trusting people are likely to look for the best in others and because of this attribute, the group also benefits as people would be socially ineffective if they constantly looked for the worst in people.

The final motive, controlling, coincides with understanding. Being able to understand another person helps an individual to predict their behavior and eventually control some aspects of the environment. Control is not necessarily a negative motive as first thought by many because control does not necessarily mean to control someone else. It is about controlling one's own actions based on what they have learned about the environment.

The five social motives have a direct connection to situationism. Situationism is described as a scientific belief that a situation impacts a person's thoughts, feelings, and behaviors, as opposed to these being solely impacted by personality. "Motives emphasize the impact of the situation as interpreted by the person. The person's motives determine the psychological situation for that person; the person-in-situation combines what is out there with the person's own motives. Thus, the core social motives determine the nature of the situation, filtered through the person's interpretations" (Fiske, 2004). According to Fiske, people generally explain people's behaviors by using their personalities as reasoning behind their actions.

Social psychology can be defined and broken down into categories and conceptual ideas, but it is basically how people start to behave like other people due to exposure to one another. Every person that exists has, at one time, posed the question of why another person or group of people act the way they do. Social psychology provides a means of explaining these behaviors that are otherwise not so easily understood.

References

Fiske, S. (2004). Social beings. Hoboken, NJ: Wiley.

Rhoda

by Jennifer J. Whitewing

Rhoda loved her dogs, twenty-seven of them. Caring for her and her son meant caring for her kennel as well. In the early summer mornings, I'd walk across the yard to the barn where the dogs were kenneled. First I'd measure kibble into the bowls of the tiny longhaired Chihuahuas, then set them free in their yard after they gobbled their chow. I'd feed the shelties, even the ones that tried to nip me, and set them free in the other two yards. Then I'd feed the white long haired Akita with the sparkling black nose who lived on a chain in the front yard. After the dogs it was time to tend to pregnant Rhoda and her 3-year-old son, Ryan.

Before abandoning the family, the husband bought an expensive red sports car. Then he drove from Montana to California. To his credit he did send money. Rhoda's doctors ordered her on bed rest for the last trimester of her pregnancy. She could get up to the bathroom, but no more. She had a history of five late term miscarriages.

I moved into her home to help. My son was her son's age and we met at church. Ryan was a beautiful child with blonde curly locks and a gleam in his eye. Little Ryan went to daycare at first, then got so violent he was expelled. He thought I had made his daddy go away. It seemed real enough to him. Dad moved out and I moved in. I was the enemy. So he was home and rebellious. He wanted his momma to get out of bed so bad he would act up just to get punished. It was a bitter scene with both of them yelling and her struggling out of bed to chase him to his bedroom and paddle him with a wooden spoon.

His room was filled with thousands of toys as his mom used to have a daycare. Every toy had its place and it overwhelmed him trying to clean up. He once said he was scared of the toys.

He also had a fascination and fear of the devil. His mother had indoctrinated him. Once Ryan and my son were taking a bath together and they intentionally splashed most of the bath water on the floor. Ryan took a curtain rod and tried to gouge my son's eye out. His behavior was sometimes terrifying.

For three months we tried to keep everyone fed and clothed. In the middle of that, we sold dogs. Dog selling involved a shampoo, drying, and brushing all the dogs that might be sold. While they were clean we kept them in the house. Some were potty trained, most were not. People came by and bought dogs for bargain prices, many having pity for Rhoda's delicate condition.

Several sales were disastrous. One Chihuahua died of a heart attack after less than one week in his new RV home. Another dog ran away in a field in town and the buyer wanted us to go find her for them. We couldn't and she was lost. A pair of dogs went to a family of 8 children and proved not housebroken. The busy, exasperated mom yelled at me about it in the supermarket. I could only shrug and empathize.

The minister's wife had a carpet cleaning business and she came out with a crew of volunteers from the church and we moved all the furniture and deep cleaned the carpets with foam. Still Rhoda wanted certain dogs in the house and messes were made, which I cleaned up. One rickety old Chihuahua really wanted to sleep with Rhoda and he left dried turds all over her bedroom. I insisted he go outside at night, so he would hide from me and we would make a game of chase with yipes and nipping.

I did the shopping for food, as well as trips to K-mart for wading pools and toys, always more things. She was on welfare and Medicaid and had a way of acquiring things on sale. She had an urgent desire to get more things.

One day as I was stocking food, I found in the freezer in the garage, entombed in a Styrofoam box, a dead fetus wrapped in plastic. It bore the address of a laboratory and I wondered if it had been autopsied there. Perfectly formed, it had frost bitten toes and fingers and was curled up in the fetal position forever resting among the frozen foods. I understood her desire to keep it and I never talked to her about it. I figured that she would bury it when the right time came. It is so hard to let go.

In the last weeks of her pregnancy Rhoda developed gestational onset diabetes. Every food had to be measured or weighed and cooked carefully. The visiting nurses came and went while I stayed to do the work. One praised me and I felt she wasn't seeing the whole imperfect picture.

When it rained the dogs would huddle in the barn or in the dog houses, but not Gizmo. Gizmo was the stud of the Chihuahuas and he would look through the glass, soaking wet, lifting one paw then the other begging to be let in. I adored Gizmo and Rhoda saw this and gave him to me as a gift to reward me for caring for the dogs.

One afternoon I ironed in Rhoda's room and we watched a movie. Little Ryan came in and jammed the tape in the VCR and broke it. He didn't mean to, but it was a loss to all of us. No more movies.

Close to nine months I drove Rhoda to the hospital with labor pains. She was sent home as it was not her time yet. One morning before dawn she came groaning across the house to awaken me and we rushed her to the hospital. We had an 18 mile drive to Bozeman and a slow truck would not let me pass. I got around him and escorted Rhoda into the hospital. We met little Ryan's babysitter in the labor room.

The nurses were quite excited. They had seen the miscarriages. One said, "Way to go Rhoda!" This time Rhoda was 10 centimeters dilated and soon gave birth to a healthy, full term, normal baby girl named Erin Rose.

I moved out as my job had ended, joyously. Her pregnancy had ended and she was no longer on bed rest. Also I had nothing left to give. I was exhausted.

Stretch to Success

by Conda V. Douglas

Nowadays much, if not most, of our daily work is done sitting at a computer. This can cause a wealth of physical problems. Besides the common carpel tunnel and tennis elbow, back and neck pain, and eyestrain, even blood clots in the legs can result from sitting for too long at a computer. There is a simple solution. This solution increases health, energy, cognitive thinking, and productivity.

Take a stretch break.

Easy. Simple. Effective. A stretch break only takes a couple of minutes to do and the rewards are far more than the cost of the effort. It's best to stretch at least every half hour or, if possible, even more often. Unlike exercises where the muscles can become too fatigued and damaged and need recovery time, there is no limit to the amount of stretching you can do on a daily basis. Stretching helps avoid the muscle inflammation that leads to tendonitis, resets the back, shoulders, and eyes to prevent strain, and moving prevents blood clots in the legs.

To get started, here are a few stretches:

Neck tilt: This is excellent for avoiding pushing your head forward which leads to eyestrain and a stiff neck. Relax your shoulders, center your head over your shoulders and then gently tilt your head to one side. Hold for three to 10 counts, Then gently bring your head back to center, pause and tilt to other side. Repeat at least three times.

Shrug: Raise and lower your shoulders three to five times, then do shoulder rolls three to five times each direction. This one is addictive.

Wrist circles: This is good for avoiding the dreaded carpel tunnel syndrome. Circle your hands, "rolling" them on your wrists, three to five times both directions. Then spread your fingers and reach out far and "grab" the treasure of good health several times. Your typing speed may increase as a result!

To get the blood moving: Stand up, walk in place for a moment, then reach your arms overhead, slightly in front of your body and alternate reaching one arm up and then the other.

These are only a few of the myriad stretches you can do throughout your writing time. If you have favorites, by all means do those as well—mix it up! Stretch when you need a mini-break. Don't just take a deep breath, STRETCH!

Texting Lessons
by Rebecca K. Grosenbach

I'm ready to admit that I'm not on the cutting edge of technology. I'm so far from cutting edge, I can't even see the edge from here. I didn't get a cell phone until 2007. My husband, Doug, and I resisted getting cell phones for our children until they started driving. "All my friends have cell phones," they insisted. To which we replied, "Then use one of theirs!"

Before sending our eldest, Abby, off to college, Doug and I broke down and bought her a cell phone. A room full of other things too, mind you, but the cell phone was a pretty big deal.

As we added Abby to our cell phone plan, we also added unlimited texting. We knew that would be an important feature for Abby. So, suddenly, I had this new communication tool at my disposal.

I have a rather dated phone and it doesn't have a full keyboard. The letters are grouped together under the number keys. The number "2" has the letters "a,b," and "c." This is nothing new; even rotary phones had letters by the numbers.

There is a snazzy feature on my phone where the phone figures out the word I want when I type in a certain combination of keys. I don't have to painstakingly type in every letter. Abby had turned on this feature (and used it) before giving me a lesson in how to use it.

One day, shortly after getting Abby her phone, I decided to send her a text message as she headed off to go shopping. I was going to write, "Hi. Have fun."

To start the word, "Hi," I hit the "4" button where the "h" is. My smart little phone spit out the word "Hi."

Sweet! I thought. *This will be really easy.*

The phone automatically put in a space and waited for the next instruction. I started typing the word "have."

"H-a-" so far so good. But then it spit out a "t" giving me "hat." It automatically gave me a space and moved on to the next word. I hit "clear" and tried again. "H-a-" and again with the "t". By this time it was beeping and flashing and I decided, *"Okay, I'll go with 'hat.' "*

"Hat fun" is almost "have fun." Abby's a smart girl. She'll figure it out.

On to the next word. I hit the "3" key three times trying to get to the "f." But the phone thought I was asking for three letters from the "3" key. So it selected "fee—" which led it naturally to the word "feet." Again, I cleared out the word and tried again. Hitting "3-3-3" gave me "feet."

I began to giggle.

Then, sitting alone in my parked car, I started to laugh.

I hit send.

"Hi. Hat feet."

Abby deftly replied, "Hat feet?"

Laughing harder, I abandoned texting and called Abby.

"Hello?" she answered.

By that time I was laughing uncontrollably, tears rolling down my face.

"Mom?"

Then Abby started to laugh, too.

I still don't text well or often. But one thing is certain—I now have a whole new way to hat feet.

Three Ways to Make Your Words Work
by Kathy McIntosh

Words are wondrous. Like music, when sung by a great voice like Placido Domingo's or played by a master, words can impel you to action or to tears or to laughter.

As a writer you want to create the desired effect: a smile or laughter when you think you're being funny, perhaps a higher pulse rate when you're creating a scary moment.

What you *don't* want is for your words to make someone laugh when you're trying to make a point. Or to irk them so much they stop reading.

Three mistakes can cause you to lose your audience or reduce your desired impact.

The first is not knowing who you are writing for. The second is too much reliance on spell checkers. A third may be caused by rushing your words into print or pixel before you've made sure they make sense and don't have glaring errors.

Know Your Audience

Even fiction writers, I propose, should know their audience. The success of Janet Evanovich (ONE FOR THE MONEY through SIZZLING SIXTEEN) owes in part to her understanding of who her audience is and what they expect in a humorous novel. She knows they want a funny, romantic, absurd romp with a happy ending. She knows her readers expect Stephanie Plum to get into trouble and to lose at least one vehicle. They expect Lula to be hungry and Grandma Mazur to be totally off the wall. Janet Evanovich knows that if you create an expectation in your audience and then change the rules, you'll disappoint them, and lose readers. That expectation is created with your first words and you should deliver on the promise until you stop writing. It helps to keep your language and style the same throughout and to use vocabulary that won't have your readers constantly thumbing through the dictionary.

Great marketers advise you to know your customer. I suggest knowing your reader and to write for that "ideal" reader.

Don't Rely Too Much on Spell Checkers

Spell checkers look for misspellings, not for misuse. Ignoring that reality can get you into all kinds of trouble.

The first trap will be homophones, or homonyms, words that sound alike but have different spellings and meanings. Steal/steel, their/they're/there, cubical/cubicle, principal/principle, reign/rein, neigh/nay, caret/carrot, lead/led, are some of my favorites.

Another spell checker oversight is the use of the wrong word. If it's a word, spell checker doesn't care. I often interchange from and form. I've seen massage in place of message, costumer instead of customer, defiantly instead of definitely, sigh language, and without instead of without. Some of these are simply amusing but some may lead your reader to a wrong conclusion or to conclude that you are not the genius you thought. I once saw a full-page ad in a local paper with a checklist to ensure safe holiday driving. If stalled it advised, "stay with your vehicle and try to converse fuel while maintaining warmth."

Don't Rush

That's a tough piece of advice. Maybe it would be more acceptable to simply advise you to be like Santa and check twice. Or thrice. It's a good idea to have someone who knows something about your topic check your work.

I once visited an upscale home's open house. The realtor's detailed color flier assured me that Wayne, not Vince or Fred, had done some extra work in one bedroom. I had to giggle. And groan. "Wayne's coating in one bedroom"? The wainscoting was nicely done. Why not the flier?

I've been invited to enjoy "taught lean turkey" sandwiches and to "commit to fitness." I received a flier in the mail that touted "Quality at Affordability!" Not only did they spell affordability wrong, what did they mean? Simply put, write in clear language that your reader will understand, set your readers' expectations and meet them, and check your work more than once. And have fun while you do it!

Unexpected Gifts
What Having Breast Cancer Gave me
by Carol S.Y. Garcia

The inside of a cancer experience is a bewildering, anxious, and tiring place. The diagnosis leaves me shaken and unsteady. My next few days and weeks are spent attending endless rounds of doctors' visits and tests. I go through the motions, doing what I am told to do next. My cancer is now running my life which has spiraled out of my control. Information is flying at me, treatment options, diagnosis details, support groups. I need to be places, make decisions, arrange for transportation, line up my insurance. All the while, I am fearful. Will they find more? Has it spread? Will I die?

People were shocked to learn I had cancer. I was the healthy one. I ate a fairly balanced diet full of vegetables (spinach and broccoli, yum!), fruits, and whole grains. I didn't drink much and I didn't smoke. I was young (50), fit, and active, running and biking regularly. And, cancer doesn't run in my family. Yes, my sister was constantly getting breast lumps checked and sometimes removed, but they were always benign. So the diagnosis of breast cancer shot out of nowhere and shattered my world.

What did I do to cause this? What brought it on? Was it the paint remover I used several years ago in my new, old house? I kept the house airy and I banished my roommate from the premises when I used it because she was "of childbearing age." Yes, I was taking all the precautions recommended on the label. Or could it be the abundance of hot dogs I ate a while back over the course of a few months? I had been unemployed for a long time and the frankfurters were on sale at a spectacular price.

I did a lot of reading and asking questions so that I could start to understand how I could be stricken with cancer. I learned that I possessed two risk factors. I started menses at a very young age (nine!) and I had never been pregnant, let alone pregnant before 35 or so. I had no control over when my period started but, hey, I could have gotten pregnant if I had any idea that might help me avoid cancer!

How does one go forward after such a stunning blow? We all find our ways. We all get hit with tragedy in one form or another and we all find our own, personal way of getting through it, or simply surviving it. I decided that if I had to experience this ordeal, I was going to get something good out of it.

Breast cancer and its treatment were now my life. Because I was single and living alone, I had to make arrangements to have someone with me for my appointments and procedures and I had to figure out how I would be cared for after surgery.

I was heavy with disappointed when my sister didn't jump on the next plane to be with me when I told her the news, but I understood on a rational level she had to be home to prepare for the visit of her college freshman son, her only child, after his first year away. No matter. I've always been self-sufficient and I would be able to cope and get through this just fine. I made arrangements with a couple of friends to take turns staying with me for the first two days after the surgery, then in just another week or so, I'd be back to work and trying to catch up on things that had fallen by the wayside during this whole whirlwind.

My Dad called, one of many he was now making to me. He'd been very attentive since I first found the lump and he didn't let the distance stand between us. He had just learned that my sister would not be coming to stay with me and he was adamant that I should not be alone. Oh, I have my friends, Dad, who are going to stay with me for a couple of days. He insisted that he would come, but since the surgery date was so close, he couldn't arrive until a week after. I was torn, and maybe even a little perturbed. A week after surgery? By then, I would be mostly back on my feet and busy catching up with things and his presence would hinder me.

A day passed as I tried to figure out how to convince my Dad he needn't come. Then I remembered my resolution, to use this experience in a positive way, to get something good out of it. I thought about how I always wanted to be closer to my Dad. He and I don't have much in common and we've struggled to bond with each other. I realized that my desire to be self-reliant was getting in the way. And so I gave myself my first gift. My Dad and I planned his visit.

It came time for my surgery and I counted my blessings for having friends who were like family, being that I have no family in town. And then one of my friends didn't come through on a promise and I was crushed. I was so crushed I thought about walking away from the friendship. By some amazing alignment of the stars, a cancer life coach had dropped into my life just a few days earlier (a miraculous gift!). Her suggestion was to look at the situation from my friend's perspective. This was hard because I was set on seeing things from my world view. But, I relented and I thought about how my friend might be feeling and I realized that she was probably distressed about my situation (duh!) and was having her own struggles with how to cope. Putting myself in her high heels created a huge shift in how I saw things. And, it helped me realize that my emotions were running amok (another duh!). With this new outlook, I was able to speak openly and lovingly to my friend about my hurt. We shared our thoughts and feelings and fears, and grew incredibly closer as a result. Can you imagine what a gift that was? A much deeper and more meaningful friendship that I will cherish my entire life.

A week after surgery, my Dad arrived. It's funny how life happens, because it turned out that I really, really needed him. On the day he arrived, I still couldn't drive, let alone go back to work. I had to rely on friends once again to help me out since I wasn't able to pick my Dad up from the airport on my own. I reached out to a couple who have been dear and close for many years. Their reaction was so heartwarming and eye opening. They had been searching for something they could do for me, but had come up dry. So when I reached out to them, they were ecstatic. Of course, they would help!

I was starting to see a pattern. I didn't reach out for help very often because I didn't want to inconvenience anyone. Sound familiar? I'd always viewed myself as being very self-reliant and self-sufficient, which can be good, in and by itself. However, I wasn't making space for other people to be there for me, to do things for me. Essentially, I was depriving my friends of the opportunity to show me how much they loved and cared for me. Having my eyes opened to this, and experiencing the outpouring of love and support were amazing gifts.

The week my Dad spent with me was one of the most special in my entire life. He doesn't cook so he took me out to eat wherever I wanted and made sure I was eating well. He also made sure I went on my daily walks and took my naps. It was a blessing to have my Dad care for me and to get to know him. And for him to know me. Ironically, he had gone through a serious medical procedure of his own over a year ago at a hospital away from his home town. I went to stay with him since my step-mom couldn't be there. However, the trip was cut short because his procedure went so well they didn't have to do a planned second procedure. I was terribly disappointed because I didn't get all of the one-on-one time with him that I was looking forward to. And now, I had him for an entire week all to myself (that never happens because there are six siblings). And to think I was going to pass this up! The time we spent together that week is one of the best gifts I will ever receive.

After my Dad left, I continued with my healing and soon started the next step of my cancer treatment which consisted of only radiotherapy. Yes! I would not have to have chemotherapy nor do the five year hormone drug therapy because I caught the cancer so early. Yes, I caught it, not the mammogram, not the doctors. If you want to give yourself a precious, potentially life saving gift, do your breast self-exams. I didn't do them regularly, nor did I exactly follow the prescribed exam regimen, but I did them when they came to mind and I did them the best I could. I may have done an exam once every few months or I may have done it several times in one month. I don't really know, but I did do them enough to know my breasts. So when I felt the tiny, miniscule granule, I knew it wasn't there before and that it was different. And that was enough.

And so I commenced my daily trips to the hospital for the radiation treatments. There would be 33 of them over the course of seven weeks. I very quickly discovered that I was one of the younger patients there (the pediatric ward is in a separate area). I was also healthier and more fit than most since I wasn't getting chemotherapy. One morning, while I was changing into the hospital gown, I heard a gasp from the dressing room next to me and I rushed over to help the elderly woman who was about to fall over. She'd had dizzy spell while attempting to change. I helped her finish changing and walked her out of the dressing area to her waiting son. That's when I realized I had stripped down to my bra! Oh, well, you see more at the beach, right?

I realized that since I was more physically able than most, perhaps I could be of help to the women who were so frail and weakened from the treatments and also to those who were also there alone and who could use a kind word and compassionate shoulder. Extending myself to others in this way gave me a sense of purpose that helped me through those 33 seemingly endless sessions. Gifts given are so often gifts received.

After the end of my radiotherapy and while I was still recovering, my mom had an emergency appendectomy. Within a few days, complications arose and things weren't looking good. She would have to stay in the hospital indefinitely and my brother, who lives in the same city as she, had an international business trip scheduled. Ordinarily, he would have canceled his trip, however, this one he couldn't because he was bound not only by a contract, but by his commitment. His withdrawal from the event, at which he was the sole presenter, would cause great dishonor to the local coordinator. He was stressed at the thought of leaving my mother alone while her condition was unstable and was torn between the two commitments. Because I was still extraordinarily fatigued from the treatment, I wasn't able to work very much and so wasn't committed to a permanent, full-time job. And, so, I jumped at the chance to help out and booked my flight as soon as I could.

The relief I felt in my brother as well as his obvious, deep appreciation brought me to tears. That I could do something so seemingly simple and have such a profound impact was enlightening. In that moment, I caught a glimpse of the load that my brother has been living with during the many years that he has been the sole offspring living near my mother. I could feel my heart expand with love and affection as a wave of overdue, truly comprehending appreciation swept over me. Understanding and appreciating others is a gift to both them and to us.

I arrived late morning, a day after my brother left on his trip. I had lunch, then took a nap. The radiotherapy took away my stamina and the travelling had wiped me out. I awoke in the late afternoon and went to the hospital. My Mom was quite upset and disappointed that I had not gotten there sooner as it was now close to her bedtime. She had not come to grips with me having cancer and so she had no concept of what condition I might be in. The next day she mostly slept and was only barely aware of my presence. Finally, on the third day, she was out of progressive care and in the regular recovery ward and more alert. I gently explained to her that I was in recovery mode and that I had to take frequent naps. She considered this, but I could tell she really didn't get it.

Like many, my Mom and I have had a difficult relationship. I felt she was domineering and controlling and I would bristle and become impatient during our exchanges. However, with the cancer recovery, I didn't have the energy to "fight" back. I was forced to take a much calmer approach. This change in the dynamics between us did wonders. My new behavior instilled a new reaction in her. Because I softened, she softened. We would talk awhile, then I would have to nap. Then she would nap. We grew closer as we recovered together. She wanted to mother me, and I welcomed it. I needed it. She needed it.

The hospital staff had set up a sleeper chair for me so that I could nap and I was also allowed to spend nights there. My mother was being closely monitored every couple of hours, so sleep there was not restful and every few days, I returned to my brother's place for the night. I would also get out and about for a couple of hours each day for some fresh air, exercise, and rejuvenation. But I now looked forward to getting back to the hospital and spending time with my Mom. After spending so much time together – this went on for almost weeks – we got to understand and appreciate each other and now our relationship is the best it has ever been. Priceless!

As adults, my brother and I simply didn't make time to visit each other (we live in different cities) and many years had gone by without us knowing each other very well. I made sure to plan my stay long enough so that I would be there for several days after he returned. It was fabulous to hang out together, to reminisce about our childhood, to meet his friends, to witness his life, and to discover who he is. Again, because of my low energy level, I was forced to be quieter – not that I'm overly talkative normally, but just the same, being quieter allowed me to listen more and to spend more time focusing on him, giving myself the gift of knowing my brother.

My relationship with my sister has always been deep and solid and I sorely missed having her with me during my treatment and my recovery. Given that I had a lot of down time during my recuperation, I pondered her absence. I also pondered her behavior during our phone calls. I'm a very direct and pragmatic person and would speak openly about the side effects of the treatment. My sister would tell me that I would be fine and then she'd say, "I'm so glad you are doing well. You sound good.", then our conversation would end. I wondered why she did not actually ask me how I was. And, yet, I would receive cards and gifts in the mail from her friends, all wishing me the best of recoveries and offering me their unbounded support. On the website that I help her with, her organization had placed pink XOXOXOs on the Home page for me. I had also seen this behavior in some of my friends.

The reactions of people to my cancer have been extremely varied. Some have cried with me, some have shared their personal stories, some have glossed over it, and some have difficulty talking about it.

With my abundance of thinking time, it dawned on me. A diagnosis of cancer in someone that you would never peg to get cancer strikes fear at our core. If she can get it, so can I. Also, the thought of cancer forces us to look at our mortality and at the mortality of our loved ones. We experience a hit to our cozy assurance that our loved ones will always be strong and healthy and alive.

I learned on a very intimate level that people process and handle fear and grief differently. My sister and my friends were grieving the fact that I had cancer. The pain for my sister was so deep, that she had to profess, "You sound good," in order to comfort not only me, but herself.

Coming to this awareness has given me huge insight into how to relate to people in difficult situations. I can better assess what might be comforting to them as opposed to what is comforting to me. To me, any additional understanding of people that I can garner which then leads to more fulfilling relationships is a gift worth chasing.

The return to full-time work has been challenging. I've experienced what's called "cancer brain fog." I've always been a high achiever and have always been able to work at an intense pace to accomplish challenging projects and to meet difficult deadlines. This ability has served me well in that I've had a wonderful career. However, this ability also has a downside. To function at that high level, I was fairly "tightly wound" as one friend called it. I am not able to function in the same way now. At first, I was incredibly distraught and frustrated. But over time, I am learning acceptance and new ways of functioning. Along the lines of opening myself up to help from my friends, I reach out for more help with my work. I have started embracing the "it takes a village" concept and have been developing deeply satisfying working partnerships with a variety of people. This is immensely rewarding and is a gift that keeps on giving!

Over the past few years, I flirted with the idea of writing a book or an inspirational article, but I never actually got around to it. And here I am, at the end of a piece that is set to be published. When I first wrote this composition, I wrote much of it in the third person. As I reviewed it for the last of many times, I realized I was ready to fully own my cancer journey and have positioned my story fully in the first person. The writing and retelling of my experiences is a gift to myself -- and perhaps to others – for it has given me another outlet to process the deep emotions that come from such a traumatic, inexplicable event.

And so I am stepping out of that bewildering, anxious, and tiring place. I own my cancer story, I share it with you, and I will become a published writer, fulfilling a long standing dream. The best gifts are unexpected and touch us deep in our hearts and are ours forever.

"You never know whom you'll influence nor when nor how."

The Freundship Column for April 19, 2005

By Jane Freund

This past week I had the opportunity to have lunch with one of my two high school English teachers. I had not seen Jo (she cringed when I called her Mrs. Young) since I graduated high school 25 years ago. Along with our mutual friend Martha, we chatted about our lives and solved many world problems (or at least thought we did). One of the joys of getting to know my teachers as adults is learning what fascinating people they are. More importantly, with the passage of time, I've had the opportunity to see the influence Jo's lessons have had on my life. Tears welled in her eyes as I thanked her for all she taught me.

Years before I had the opportunity to tell my other high school English teacher, Sue Mousseau, how much she had influenced my life. Tears welled in her eyes as well, but the circumstances were much different than with Jo.

As part of our 20-year high school reunion, we invited all of our high school teachers to join the festivities. I was particularly hopeful that Sue would be able to come as I knew she had been ill. I was disappointed when she declined our invitation. Then during the reunion, her son Jack (who was a classmate of mine) asked that I come to his parents' house that Sunday so that I could see his Mom. I was deeply touched and readily accepted the invitation.

I suspect that the Lord humors me but I try to prepare myself for any situation I'm about to face. Well nothing could have prepared me for seeing Sue. The illness that had gripped her was "frozen face" Parkinson's disease. I had always known Sue as an active, energetic individual and now she had little, if any, control over her facial expressions. At the age of 62, she was trapped in her own body. I nearly cried when I helped her put on her shoes because she could not do so herself.

Another very poignant moment was when I told her how much she had influenced me. I told her I would not have become a writer if not for her encouragement. Tears welled up in her eyes and in mine as well. As I hugged her goodbye, I knew I would probably never see her again and I was right.

"You never know whom you'll influence nor when nor how." I don't remember who eulogized Sue at her funeral, but that quote of hers stuck with me from the moment I heard the words and wrote them on the back of the program. As part of my e-mail signature, those words have gone out in thousands of e-mails I've sent. Her influence continues.

Speaking of influence, I want to share part of an e-mail sent to me by Sheryl, a high school classmate and friend of mine. If you ever wonder how even the smallest actions can affect somebody else, read about "Susan" (not her real name) and Sheryl's contact with her during our 20-year reunion:

"Although Susan didn't graduate (she quit school in our senior year) she came to the Friday night cocktail party at the Shiloh Inn and told me why she quit school... She couldn't read! When Susan met the man who is now her husband, I believe in 1981, he taught her to read. She then told me that I had a lot to do with her wanting to learn how to read. I always had a book with me when we were in high school. It may have been a best-selling novel or a trashy romance novel, but I always had a book and I would pull it out of my purse and read. Susan said that she always wanted to be able to do that, but hadn't learned how. She and I talked on the phone on Saturday afternoon before the Reunion Dinner, which she wasn't attending, and talked about books that we both had read and it was wonderful."

"You never know whom you'll influence nor when nor how."

God in my Life

A Cracked Pot

by Lynette Sali

broken splintered
dry, cracked, imperfect pot
depressed, sad, hopeless, angry
unwell, injured, ugly, overwhelmed
abused, neglected, beaten down, unloved
criticized, judged, discouraged, despairing
scorned, rejected, separated, isolated, lonely
fearful, heartbroken, relationships in discord
defeated, victim mentality, unmet expectations
wild, compulsive, addicted, in denial, confused
an anxious perfectionist, dysfunctional failure
I'm broken in spirit, a doubting distrust nags
I run into the arms of nurturing Father God
snug in unconditional love and acceptance
I can honestly accept self in my "now"
As I dig to unearth my naked truth
I reach for recovery
hungry for healing
thirsty
empty
waiting to be filled

WRITER'S NOTE: This poem turned into a piece of art as I continued to add to it. I sat back in my chair to think. With squinted eyes I looked at the computer screen and realized there appeared to be a "crack" in the pot. I played with the spacing and a cracked pot appeared.

I wrote "A Cracked Pot" during a time of great brokenness when I did not think I would ever find healing. Poetry and art were therapeutic as I sought to find God in my brokenness.

I was a broken pot. After years of depression, dysfunction, and pain, God opened the doors for help from a Christian psychologist and a gifted counselor/social worker to unravel the twisted vines of my past. I learned God loves me just like I am (in my "now") and would walk with me, at my pace, as I healed.

Most of us are broken somewhere and it was a balm to my heart to realize that someday my journey will take on meaning when I can pass on the comfort that God has given me to someone else who is hurting.

One of my life verses is 2 Corinthians 1:3-4
3All praise to God, the Father of our Lord Jesus Christ. God is our merciful Father and the source of all comfort. 4He comforts us in all our troubles so that we can comfort others. When they are troubled, we will be able to give them the same comfort God has given us. **(New Living Translation of the Bible)**

God's unconditional love and acceptance are a refuge for me. After years as a Christian, I finally understand at a deeper level that I don't have to earn His love. God will repair the cracks and fill you and me to overflowing with His love and peace. Then our pots will hold water once more and we can pour out "Living Water" for others.

He heals the brokenhearted and binds up their wounds. Psalm 147:3

...*for He satisfies the thirsty and fills the hungry with good things.* Psalm 107:9

Angels in Philadelphia

by Gena Shikles

I don't know if you believe in angels, but I believe that we met one in Philadelphia many years ago.

We were planning a family vacation over the fourth of July. We were meeting my folks in Pennsylvania for a few days. Ernie, my husband, was sent off on a business trip right before the vacation and so he made plans to meet up with our daughter, Christina, and me in Philadelphia on Friday night. We would pick him up at the airport.

Christina and I took off from Roanoke and had no problems. We had a road atlas and followed it up to Pennsylvania. All went well until we got on the turnpike. I had not been able to pick up a state map and I had no idea where the airport was in Philadelphia. I was somewhat anxious about stopping at the truck stop on the turnpike since it was late in the evening, but I knew we had to have some directions to find the airport. Christina and I went inside and couldn't find a map to buy, but there was a large map posted on the wall. I started to figure out the best way.

Several others were trying to find directions and I struck up a conversation with a family nearby. The man was from Philadelphia and showed me exactly where the airport was, the best way to get there, and then told me to follow him the remainder of the way – he'd help to get us there. He lived one exit past the airport.

We followed our angel the last of the way into Philadelphia. He took us right to the airport exit and honked and flashed his lights so I would know it was the place to get off. I drove right in and there at the first gate was Ernie waiting for us to pick him up.

Assertive Life Balance
by Taffy Pullin

Assertiveness is such a hard issue for me.
I struggle to know what is right.
I know I need to stand up for myself.
Sometimes it's an exhausting inner fight.

I need a healthy respect and view of myself.
Some call it self-acceptance, self love, or self esteem.
The point is not to lose my "self" living life
When I'm passive life loses its gleam.

I once served to get praise and approval,
Labored to achieve perfection and applause.
I eventually exhausted myself and collapsed,
Even I didn't realize the root cause.

I gave out of a needy soul's emptiness.
I found I performed to please.
And I lost my "self" in the process
And my heart was never at ease.

I heard the pastor say "you must die to self".
I tried my best but the pain was intense.
I found it unhealthy to "die to self" when I didn't have one,
To heal and develop a healthy sense of "self" made sense.

Depression hovered and hounded.
I was a very depressed mother and bride.
It took years to heal the wounds and trauma
That had warped imbedded false beliefs inside.

I began my journey to emotional and spiritual wholeness,
To heal deep heart issues and develop a healthy sense of "self".
I'm learning to honestly and firmly express my needs and desires.
When I take assertive action to be healthy, life will balance itself.

Whatever my situation in life,
Inner value and true refreshment come from above.
The Lord wants healthy decisions involving self care,
They are crucial to serve the Lord with a pure love.

The Bible tells me to be a servant,
To die to self and turn the other cheek.
I know the Lord thinks I have value.
Jesus was strong, yet He was meek.

Meekness is strength under control,
Not <u>always</u> demanding one's way.
There is a time and a place to assert myself.
Lord, give me wisdom in my walk each day.

I know I need to pick my battles
And stand up for what is important to me,
For I am a unique person of value
And the Lord wants me to walk free.

I find I often second guess myself,
It's exhausting to know what to do.
He's showing me that I can still be "me"
While serving God and ministering to my family crew.

Sometimes family members have so many wants and needs.
They forget I'm a person and my needs get put on a shelf.
If another does not choose to nourish me,
I must plug into the Lord and take care of myself.

I once thought meeting my own needs was selfish,
Then realized no one person can ultimately fulfill every need.
Intimacy with the Lord, activities, interests, and friends all help
If it's balanced, it is a healthy thing to do indeed!

It's up to me to fill my tank to maintain balance
So fatigue, anger, and bitterness don't set in.
I finally realize that the Lord wants me healthy
And it's OK to meet my needs within.

Answers come with a balanced approach.
Time with the Lord to strengthen and refresh is the key.
Time away, time with friends, time for fun
Are the things that will make a healthy "me."

A healthy "me" can serve others well.
Now "dying to self" does not take me out.
I want other wounded, passive women to know
Joy comes as we heal and grow from the inside out.

As I work to heal the wounded parts within,
I'm finding a precious woman with a true servant heart.
A healthy "self" can genuinely serve others,
Assertive life balance is a goal we must embrace and impart.

Box

by Janet Strong

I am prone to wonder:
are you really there,
do you really care?
I want to
put you in box
so I can understand you.
But you pop
the lid every time,
and refuse
to be contained.

Calvary Love

by Terry Brown

Your love is safe - secure
Your love is overflowing - lavishing
It is like the ocean rolling over my wounded, shriveled heart

Your love is costly – His blood that bought me
Your love is cleansing – never ending
Washing away all my sin and stain making me whole again

Your love drives away my fears
It wipes away my tears
It surrounds me – even hounds me
Till I receive it with open arms

Oh Calvary love, what marvelous love was poured out for me!
There's no greater love than Calvary love.

Your love is selfless, has my best interest in mind
It is one of a kind
Your love's engaging, never raging
Its unending toward me for all time

Your love chases me, embraces me
Reaching me and teaching me to love like no other love

Oh Calvary love, what marvelous love was poured out for me,
Poured out for me

So I ask Thee, please now flow through me
Your love to a lost and hurting world
So in need of Calvary love, flow through one
Flow through me – for Calvary love has changed me!!

Chrysalis Transformation

by Lynette Sali

I, too, began life as an egg
I grew . . .
A worldly, ravenous caterpillar
Salvation came. . .
Then a chrysalis of God's agape love,
A protective growth cocoon
And miraculous inner transformation.

Behold . . .I emerge
. . .a new creation
. . . a beautiful butterfly!

I fly . . . . .free.

Author's Note: When I think of being a new creation in Christ, the butterfly always comes to mind. What an incredible transformation takes place inside the chrysalis! Like the butterfly, a Christian's growth is internal before one can see or experience a transformed life.

Although the "old me" has gone, the "new me" must be molded and shaped so that I can hopefully reflect the image of Christ Jesus.

In studying the monarch butterfly as I wrote this piece, I found out the butterfly's life span is only two weeks. Before the butterfly dies, it lays eggs and the cycle begins again. To me this represents spiritual growth, as God continues to place me in "spiritual chrysalis" situations to further transform me into His image.

I'm filled with joy every time I see a butterfly because it reminds me that I am God's creation, too. In the "Sonlight " of His love, I grow and bloom into something beautiful in His time.

"Therefore, if anyone is in Christ, he is a new creation; the old has gone, the new has come!" 2 Corinthians 5:17

Comfort for my Empty Arms

by Lynette Sali

My empty arms are aching, my heart is tattered and torn
I yearn for God's tender comfort as the death of my child I mourn.
For I lost a tiny one dear to me; the pain is very real;
Yet the Lord is close beside me as my emotions start to heal.

Though I lift my arms toward heaven and release that tiny soul to God above,
I still long for a comforting embrace from the Lord...it comes in the form of love.
The love of family and friends surround me as they share my sorrow and pain;
And I know someday soon I will feel life is worth living again.

When I envision my baby held tenderly in Jesus' loving arms,
The pain doesn't grip so tightly, and I realize he's safe from harm.
When I think of my precious baby, my empty arms still ache with sorrow;
Yet I know deep in my heart that God loves me, and there will be a brighter tomorrow.

The healing God gave to my tiny one is the ultimate freedom from sickness and pain,
For the soul of my babe is with Jesus, and I can thank Him in spite of my pain.
As I picture God rocking my wee one in His heavenly rocking chair,
I am reassured again just how special it is to know God's loving care.

If I ask He will give me comfort and peace that no man understands.
And I look toward the day when I'll see my child--when my own earthly life ends.
The reunion will be a sweet one as I see his tiny face.
I can picture the joy and serenity as we enjoy God's love and grace.

Even though my heart is broken, I sense God's love deep within.
He is always right beside me; His healing touch won't let me cave in.
He helps me look to the future for what He has in mind.
For whatever He has planned for me, I know His joy I'll find.

But for now I ask for His comfort for my empty, empty arms;
And I ask that He constantly guide me and keep me safe from harm.
I know His peace and comfort will heal my broken heart.
For I need His strength and courage to make a brand new start.

As I think of the Lord as my comforter, 2 Corinthians 1:3-5 comes to mind.
For as He comforts me in my sorrow, I, in turn, can comfort those in a bind.
For my sorrow can be turned to triumph when I reach out in love to another,
And am able to share God's comfort with a hurting sister or brother.

So as my trials mold and shape me into the person He desires,
His peace and comfort are the fuel that feeds my Godly desires.
For, above all, I seek to revere Him in all I say and do.
And I realize, again, that in every situation, I can honor Him with what I do.

Empty Arms

By Lynette Sali

We were excited about the promise of a new life.
Then, unexpectedly, our baby was……just…..gone……..

Becoming a mother is a unique, miraculous experience. Whether you feel the baby move or kick within, give birth, or hold a precious, chosen child through adoption, you and your family's life is forever changed if you lose that precious little one.

OUR STORY

I became pregnant with a third child while an IUD was in place. The doctor removed the IUD and everything seemed fine. Though the pregnancy was a surprise to us, it was not a surprise to God. We were excited to welcome this little one. My husband Greg (aka Daddy) patted my growing tummy and talked and sang to the little one growing within me. Then I became ill with pneumonia and was put on strong antibiotics. At 10-12 weeks in the pregnancy I started spotting and cramping. My obstetrician advised I rest and take it easy.

Though it has been almost 30 years ago, I clearly remember the pain and shock of that day. As it was my day to drive the carpool and I was not one to shirk my responsibilities, I planned to drive and then rest after I returned home. Despite increasing pain, I made it to the car and began the drive to pick up children and deliver them to school. After I dropped them off, I began to experience waves of intense pain with cramps. The cramps intensified and began to feel like labor contractions. The drive home became a white-knuckled trip as I gripped the steering wheel and tried to breathe when each pain hit. I lay down to rest, but nothing helped. A short time later I delivered a tiny baby. Ironically, this was the only baby I actually delivered "naturally," as our two sons had been caesarean births. I delivered a BABY, a tiny human so small he fit in the palm of my small hand. There was NO doubt in my mind that I had miscarried a precious baby.

My husband Greg came home from work to comfort me. As wrote this article, we relived that day and talked about how the miscarriage had affected each of us. I know now the loss of our baby affected him much more than I had thought. In listening to him, I realized the miscarriage had cracked his rough exterior and touched his heart and emotions. He remembered his coming home had meant a lot to me. As he thought about our life over 30 years ago, he said, "I was a military man and my comfort sometimes seemed like an uncaring stone." As Greg held our baby, he put his arm around me and prayed for comfort and healing. It was a painfully sweet moment, as he was grieving too.

We took turns gently cradling our baby in our hands. I remember vividly how very small he was, his features so perfect he looked like he was simply asleep, snuggled in his Daddy's hands. Greg remembers thinking he looked like he was sitting on the heel of his hand. Greg's cupped fingers supported his back, and his tiny head was bowed as if he were praying. He was beautiful, perfect in every way, with arms and legs, ten fingers and ten toes, dark spots where his eyes were developing, ear buds, a nub for a nose, and a delicate little mouth with a Mona Lisa smile of peace. His daddy remembers his unique God-designed palm prints and footprints, already visible even though he had been in my womb less than three months.

Greg and I continued to talk through the miscarriage as I wrote. He remembers holding the baby and asking him, "Why?" as it seemed he might lift his little head to look in his Daddy's eyes and answer. When the baby did not respond, Greg asked God an anguished, "WHY?" The miscarriage was so very hard to understand, as the baby seemed to be so perfect. The Holy Spirit spoke to Greg's heart and said, "All babies are mine. All life is mine and I decide when to call them home."

Greg sought solace in God's word and was reminded of Matthew 10:29 "…not a single sparrow can fall to the ground without your Father knowing it." (New Living Translation ©2007) Knowing God cares about a single sparrow, we then understood at a deep level that He knew and loved our baby. And He knew about our broken hearts and cared about us as we grieved our loss.

My doctor had no explanation for my miscarriage. There was no way to know if the IUD or the antibiotics had caused it. I have since learned miscarriage, though unexpected, is not uncommon. A miscarriage is defined as an unexpected loss prior to the 20th week of pregnancy, often ending a pregnancy when the baby is not developing normally. My doctor wanted to see the baby and tissue that I had passed to make sure the entire placenta had been expelled. If not, a D and C procedure would be necessary. So I headed to the doctor's office and handed over the bag of "fetal tissues." Medical people confirmed that I had passed the entire placenta. My doctor said I was OK and advised we wait three months for my body to heal and get back to normal before trying to get pregnant again.

That was the last time I saw my little one. Oh, how I wish I had taken a picture, though the pictures in my mind are likely more vivid and they can never be misplaced or damaged. In looking back, I also wish we had asked for his little body to be returned to us, so we could have honored his short life through cremation or burial. I was in so much shock at the time, it did not even occur to me to ask.

Our empty arms ached, and the grief was so fresh that we didn't know if we wanted to try again for a third child. We were still praying about it when I found out a little over three months later that I was pregnant again. We were excited, though I have to admit I did have fear that I would miscarry again or that something might be wrong with the baby.

My wise husband reminded me that God is in control. He reflected on Psalm 139:13:

"… For You created my inmost being; You knit me together in my mother's womb." (The Holy Bible, New International Version). He reassured me, reminding me that God had knit together the baby we lost. If God chose to give us another baby, He would give me the strength to handle any outcome. I later learned most women suffering one miscarriage can expect to have normal future pregnancies.

And that's the way it was for us. We joyously welcomed a daughter the following year. We named her Carolyn, which means "Joyful Spirit." I spent many hours nursing, holding and rocking her, and Greg loved to fall asleep with her skin-to-skin on his chest, just as he had done with our boys.

We especially treasured Carolyn's birth after our loss. Our miscarriage had changed Greg and me forever, especially our views on abortion. No longer could we accept that a miscarriage was "a blob of fetal tissue" after we had held in our hands a tiny, beautiful human being only 10-12 gestational weeks old. Our experience has confirmed in our hearts that life <u>does</u> begin at conception.

The loss of any child is traumatic, particularly the loss of a tiny, tiny innocent baby. The loss of a child through miscarriage (loss of a baby less than 20 weeks gestation), stillbirth (gestation age of 20 weeks through a full term pregnancy), an infant's death soon after birth, Sudden Infant Death Syndrome, fatal illness, or accidental/unusual deaths are all traumatic losses that leave birth and adoptive parents heartbroken and bewildered. The mother who carried/cared for the child wonders what she could have done to prevent the baby's death. Whatever the circumstances and reasons for the loss, the entire family is left with broken hearts and empty arms.

The loss of a baby by miscarriage or through abortion is a loss that is not officially recognized in our society. Some states do issue a Fetal Death Certificate for the miscarriage of a baby under 20 weeks gestation, though usually no death certificate is issued. Fetal Death Certificates for aborted babies remain a controversial issue.

In the minds of many, no acknowledgement of a death prior to 20 weeks gestation also means no acknowledgement of a "life." Usually, no one will report or read a death announcement or an obituary, attend a memorial service or burial, or have a special place to visit, grieve, or place a flower. These little ones are unknown, unacknowledged babies in our society, but certainly not unknown or uncared about by the God who created them and the family who lost them. A pregnancy or adoption after birth is the promise of a new life, with the expectation of holding a baby in your arms. When that precious baby dies, the heartache is deep.

Intense pain, grief, and guilt may engulf a woman who, years before, chose to have an elective abortion. As she tries to heal, accept God's forgiveness, and forgive herself, her cries of pain may fall on deaf ears and uncompassionate hearts. Actually, the reason for the loss of the baby is not the issue. All share the pain and grief of loss and recovery can be a lonely journey.

RESOURCES TO HELP

Years ago, parents of stillborn babies received a Death Certification, but no Birth Certificate. That is changing due to the efforts of Arizona resident Joanne Cacciatore, PhD, MSW, FT, and mother of a stillborn baby. After the stillbirth of her daughter Cheyenne, Dr. Cacciatore went on to establish the MISS Foundation, a nonprofit corporation committed to helping families discover hope and eventually heal from the trauma of a child's death. According to information on the MISS website, more than 120,000 children die every year in the United States. Of those, more than 80% die before their first birthday.

In an article published in 2007, Christine Vestal featured Joanne's story:

> "My stillborn baby was the prettiest baby of all of my five children. She looked perfect. She was so well-nourished she had rolls of fat around her cheeks and knees. But she never took a breath and never made a sound," said Arizona resident Joanne Cacciatore.
>
> "After I left the hospital, I got her death certificate in the mail, and they told me state law required me to bury or cremate the body," Cacciatore said. But Arizona never issued a birth certificate. "How can you have a death, if you never have a birth?" she asked.
>
> In 1994, "after the stillbirth of her daughter Cheyenne, Cacciatore set out to change her state's policy and launched a nationwide organization of parents seeking state-issued birth certificates for stillborn babies.

> In 2001, Arizona became the first state to enact a law giving parents the option of receiving a certificate of birth for a still-born baby.

Largely through the efforts of Cacciatore grassroots organization — the MISS Foundation — 20 states now offer parents of stillborn babies the option of an official birth certificate -- 19 by law and one, Georgia, by administrative policy. Of those states, Arizona, Indiana and Missouri also provide state income-tax deductions for the year of the stillbirth to help defray burial expenses. In the laws, the gestation period at which a fetal death is considered a stillbirth rather than a miscarriage varies among states, with some starting as early as 20 weeks."

Information on the MISS website states: "Every state in the U.S. already issues a death certificate for all stillbirths. Additionally, each state has a final disposition mandate for stillbirths. Many parents want to have their child's birth certificate in addition to their death certificate. Unfortunately, without legislative change, most states are unable to accommodate the parents' wishes." The above article reported that more states were to introduce legislation. The MISS Foundation continues to work with states to enact MISS-ing Angels legislation which will allow for the issuance of a "Certificate of Birth Resulting in Stillbirth."

http://www.missfoundation.org/index.html, the M.I.S.S Foundation's website, offers many supportive resources including a Newsletter, a Father's Page, and a Cherish Corner where people can post about their loss. The online "Forums" contain 27 online support groups with thousands of members. The website also features information on many subjects including finding a therapist, sibling grief, planning a funeral, the healing process, and ways to remember your child. Dr. Cacciatore facilitates a therapeutic healing event, The Barefoot Walkabout, that has helped many.

> The Walkabout is a grief coping strategy discovered by Dr. Joanne Cacciatore in 2007. The journey involves the concept of Mindfulness. "Mindful grieving is being fully present, in the moment, with the mourning experience, nonjudgmentally with our own emotions and the emotions of others. This mode of being with grief includes unconditional acceptance of where we are in that particular moment."
>
> "For those are spiritual or religious, the walkabout is an opportunity to be in both silence and solitude with God. Some of Dr. Cacciatore patients feel they've experienced an encounter with God during their own silent walkabout. Others have merely felt the grounding of the experience with the Earth. For the secular, it's an opportunity to allow nature to teach about the journey of grief. Either way, the Barefoot Walkabout facilitates an encounter with meaning in a profound way for many.
>
> The Barefoot Walkabout is an intentional practice of being fully present, in the moment, with our current state of mind and heart. It's a journey no one will ever forget."
>
> Dr .Cacciatore hope is that"a woman will "discover something new about herself and the process of mourning."

In another recent internet search, I also found wonderful information from HopeXchange, an expanding company with the primary goal of offering support to those coping with miscarriage, stillbirth, or infant death. Their guiding maxim is "shining light on pregnancy loss." Easily accessible, the website http://www.hopexchange.com contains a wide variety of articles, books, music, and resources including information on causes and myths about miscarriage, help with grief, depression and anger, and information on future pregnancies.

According to data adapted from the book *Hope is Like the Sun: Finding Hope and Healing After Miscarriage, Stillbirth, or Infant Death* by Lisa Church, the HopeXchange website posted these statistics: "...approximately 1 in 4 pregnancies end in miscarriage; and some estimates are as high as 1 in 3. If you include loss that occurs before a positive pregnancy test, some estimate that 40% of all conceptions result in loss....An estimated 80% of all miscarriages are single miscarriages."

The Story Behind The Poem "Comfort For My Empty Arms"

When I miscarried in 1980, there were few resources to help people heal after the loss of a baby. The internet was not yet in existence. Few talked openly about their grief and loss. A few years after my miscarriage, I attended the funeral of an infant who had lived only a few days. That event caused me to revisit our loss. I worked through another level of grief as I wrote the poem, "Comfort for my Empty Arms." As I pictured "God rocking my wee one in His heavenly rocking chair," I felt God wrap His soft, warm blanket of comfort around me. Though I grieved, I knew my baby was safe in the arms of Jesus. I sent a copy to the parents who had just buried their newborn, and have continued to share the poem with many who have lost a baby.

When I tell my story to someone who has had a miscarriage or stillbirth before their due date, I tell them about the after effects of my miscarriage. I was irritable, angry, depressed, and out of sorts, especially as the baby's due date approached. Close to my due date, I was especially irritated by the very pregnant lady complaining about her discomfort. Her comments hurt and felt like salt being rubbed into an open wound. I would gladly have traded places with her.

I finally connected the dots when I learned that my emotions, feelings, confusion, distorted thinking, and inability to cope were part of unresolved trauma. They are signals the loss has not been resolved and the pain healed and that one's grief must be recognized and processed. If possible, I share my story with both the mother and the father so they know what to expect. Then they are not surprised if the marriage is stressed, emotions flare, depression increases, and/or they have some anger at pregnant women around the time of the baby's due date. My hope is that they seek help to heal.

Anger is just part of the grieving process, and seeing someone holding a baby or someone who is close to delivery can trigger the grief. Those who have miscarried or have lost children may find due dates or birthdays difficult. When the pain of loss is still fresh or the loss has yet to be healed, a woman who has lost a child may find it painfully difficult to go to church on Mother's Day when mothers are honored. Fathers can experience the same feelings of loss of Fathers' Day, the due date, or the birthday.

A Healing Journey simply takes time, and strong feelings will rise and fall as one walks out her own unique journey. The absence of your baby will leave a hole in your heart and you will never forget. And you may think you are fine and have put the loss behind you, only to have it surface many years later. Journaling has been very therapeutic for me as I worked through life issues.

In my case, I was surprised that 30 years later, while in counseling for other issues, unhealed pockets of grief surfaced. My counselor took me another level deeper to realize that there was still emotional trauma and pain from the miscarriage that needed resolution. Although I was surprised that there was still so much pain, I was older and more mature and ready to do the work of recovery. . . . . ready to face, feel, and grieve the loss. Was it easy? No, but the sweet fruit of the work I did is a heart that is healed and whole.

The loss of your child will always be a major event in your life. The loss changes the life you once knew, and has the capability to negatively affect you if you do not heal. I encourage you to consider professional counseling to help you heal, especially if you continue to struggle emotionally or unresolved grief causes you to have trouble coping with life. Staying "stuck" can become another issue to overcome, so take advantage of the many resources available locally and on the internet.

As your heart heals, the pain lessens and no longer defines or controls you. You will learn to integrate your loss into your life. The day will come when you are able to talk about the loss of your baby and tell your story without the deep pangs of grief and sharp stab of pain to your heart. You will feel whole instead of hollow.

Someday you may have an opportunity to share your story to encourage another who is deep in grief from the loss of a baby. I have learned that the hard things in my life are the very areas where God uses me. Those who have been wounded and have healed are the best counselors and supporters. When you have walked that road, YOU KNOW . . . . . the one in pain does not even have to explain. You know not only the pain and sorrow, but can give them hope that healing is possible. Sharing your journey brings hope to them and joy to you, as you pass on or "pay forward" the comfort and support you once received from God and others.

We believe we will see our baby again when we get to heaven, and we look forward to that day. I sometimes envision my child running into my arms when he sees me. What a sweet reunion that will be for Greg, me, and our children For now, I know in my heart I am to continue to reach out, comfort, encourage, and support those who have empty arms.

Sources:

1. The Holy Bible, New International Version ©
2. The Holy Bible, New Living Translation ©2007
3. M.I.S.S. Foundation, http://www.missfoundation.org/index.htm
4. Vestal Christine, "Stillborn laws entangled in abortion debate," Stateline.org Staff Writer, May 17, 2007 **HTTP://WWW.STATELINE.ORG/LIVE/DETAILS/STORY?CONTENTID=208701**

Doin' His Stuff (in response to BSF study of John)

by Lynette Sali

God is the great I AM
Who wants His child to be
A living example of His love.
Am I willing to be the only Jesus they see?

I am my Father's child.
I am submitted, equipped to be
A functioning part of His Body,
Allowing Jesus to minister through me.

I am filled with the Spirit;
I am grafted into the vine of love.
I am strengthened with His power;
I am humbly poured out for others in love.

Spiritual discernment, wisdom, and understanding
Allow me to walk in His mercy and grace.
I am empathy's healing touch;
I encourage others to look in His face.

I am His ears that hear;
I am His eyes that see.
I am God's healing balm;
In meeting others' needs, I am set free.

I am His hands that serve;
I am His feet that walk where He leads.
I am His voice that speaks,
Planting His spiritual truth seeds.

I am His outstretched arms,
That comfort in pain and sorrow
I am God's love in action
"Doin' His Stuff" today and tomorrow.

We love because He first loved us. I John 4:19

Giving Into God
by Tina Frederick

I fell to my knees and my heart cried out, "Alright! Alright! I give!"
With so much pain and hurt inside I screamed out, "You win"
"I can't do this on my own; I just can't fix it, God."
"Take this burden off my heart so I won't feel this pain again."

"My way only made it worse and sorrow I can't bear.
I give it to You, do as You wish, my life is yours to command.
Take this pain away from me and let my poor heart breath,
Whatever You want, whatever You wish, my life is in Your hands."

I fell down sobbing all the tears I'd held back for so long,
Then I felt His arms around me and felt the Spirit near.
He whispered, "Precious child, I've loved you through it all."
As He held me close I poured out all the anger, pain, and fear.

I lay there and let Him hold me, kept in his Embrace
Feeling a sense of happiness I had never felt before.
My anger became forgiveness, my sorrow turned to hope.
He whispered, "This is just the start, for you I have much more."

Satisfaction

by Janet Strong

No longer tilling to eat
instead, idle hands, wondering minds.
Trouble and vain endeavors
looking good on the outside,
empty within.
Productivity does not satisfy
Creativity helps for a moment
Exercise calms for a time
Fellowship can touch the heart
But still you are not satisfied.
Love the King of the universe.
Be diligent to give grace to your fellow man
Take your thoughts and hold them captive to truth
Choose every breath to praise the Savior.
This is soul satisfaction until
We are in eternity with Him.

Strength

by Janet Strong

It may seem impossible,
bigger than you ever imagined.
School, relationships, or work
may be more than you think you can handle.
But if God called you to the task,
He will give you strength,
One moment at a time,
You can rest in Him.

Thanksgiving Psalm
by Gina Burns

I walk in the morning, Lord,
And smell the air, fresh with dew.
I feel your presence in your creation, dear Father,
And my heart swells with love for you
As I consider all the many blessings you bring.
Praise you, God, for giving us shelter;
Praise you, God, for giving us food.
Praise you, Holy One, for our loved ones.
Praise you, for all that is good comes from you.

Sometimes the news of this world
Will encroach and threaten me.
When I hear the sadness and torment that some endure,
My heart breaks and I feel afraid.
Sometimes I am assailed with doubt and
Question my worthiness to be your child.

You always reach through my fear, dear God.
You remind me that I am your child;
You knew me before I was born.
You are not a Father who abandons His children;
You are a Father of endless mercy, forgiveness, and love.

I will love you always, Lord.
I will praise your name on earth
And in Heaven.
I will join the angels and saints in singing our love for you
For all time.

The Love I Grew Up With

by Terry Brown

The love I grew up with was so unsure and caused me to question – do I deserve it? Maybe I'm not "good enough".

Maybe I don't try hard enough to do all I could. Do you really care? Does your love really care?

The love I grew up with would come and go on a whim. It was up, then it was down. It went away – not here to stay.

The love I grew up with was demanding, so demanding. When expectations weren't met it let me know disappointment, frustration, and exasperation – I'm not good enough!!

The love I grew up with provided for external needs – food, shelter, and clothing.

It lacked the deeper needs – assurance (all would be ok), acceptance (you're ok), alliance (I'm with you, we're a team, I'll never leave).

This love I grew up with was confusing; sometimes there was a hug, but then a slap across the face.

The love I grew up with was fragile, so fragile. Life's trials broke it in pieces. We had to try and pick up its fragments on our own, so alone.

The wind seemed to blow it away, love doesn't last, love isn't safe. I must not be lovable, I must not be worth it.

"Greater love has no man than this, that he lay down his life for his friends." John 15:13

"But God demonstrates His love for us in that while we were still sinners Christ died for us." Romans 5:8

(God loves the unlovely) (He thinks we are worth it!)

The Smiling Heart
by Lynette Sali

Our then four-year-old grandson, Gabriel (Gabio), had a nasty cut on his cheek. As Mom and Dad bandaged it up, they asked what happened. He said he had hit it on the kitchen floor tile. The explanation didn't quite make sense, but they didn't press the issue.

The next day their Bapa was visiting and casually asked Gabio, "How did you hurt your cheek?"

His big sister Brianna, a kindergartner, quickly piped up, "He cut it on the pizza cutter."

That surprising truth obviously explained why they had not been honest with their parents, as they had been told not to play with knives and sharp things. Their Daddy wasn't at home at the time, so Bapa took the opportunity to talk to Gabio about not telling the truth. He led Gabio through the process of apologizing to his mother and asking her forgiveness. Bapa then asked him how his heart felt.

He replied, "My heart is smiling now!"

"And what was your heart feeling before you apologized to your mommy?" asked Bapa.

"My heart was sad," replied Gabio seriously.

"Who do you think wants your heart to be happy?" Bapa inquired.

"Jesus!" was the quick reply.

So conversation continued and a few minutes later Brianna said "I need to apologize to Mommy, too, 'cause I want my heart to be smiling, too." She knelt down in front of her mother and proceeded to say she was sorry for not telling the truth about what happened. Then to Mommy and Bapa's surprise, she continued, "And I need to tell you something else. Gabio and I were playing tag with the pizza cutter and he fell when he was chasing me with the pizza cutter. That's how he cut his cheek."

A short safety lesson was followed by a warning about the dangers of playing "pizza cutter tag." Brianna was now reconciled to her mommy. Then Bapa asked Brianna, "How does your heart feel now?"

"Oh, it feels happy again!" she announced with a big smile.

That sweet lesson illustrating the confession, forgiveness, and reconciliation process is now etched on the hearts of those two sweet children. May our hearts always end up smiling as we humble ourselves to admit we are wrong, ask for forgiveness, and seek to reconcile relationships we hold dear, especially that intimate relationship we have with our Lord Jesus.

Through the Fog
Finding God in the Heartbreak of Miscarriage

by Rebecca K. Grosenbach

When my husband, Doug, and I were first married, we were in no hurry to have children. But after a few years we decided that if we were going to have a family, we'd better get started. We soon realized there are some things in life you can't schedule. Five years went by. Then eight.

But then, one day, the home pregnancy test was positive—we were going to have a child! I imagined my burly husband cradling a tiny baby in his arms. I mentally redecorated our spare room with pictures of lively jungle animals. But within a matter of weeks our excitement turned to sadness when the baby failed to thrive and I miscarried.

The paint peeled from my virtual nursery. I'd catch myself staring blankly into space when I was supposed to be listening to a conversation. At work I'd read the same words over and over again without comprehension.

I didn't really ask why this had happened to me. I knew bad things happened to everybody. I'd grown up going to church and committed my life to Jesus Christ as a child. But now I wondered if it was God who sustained me or was it merely my belief in God?

Could I believe in some nebulous supreme being and find the strength I needed? Could I pull myself up by my own bootstraps and make it through the hard times? Or was Jesus Christ a genuine source of strength in my life?

Then one day sitting alone in my office, I found myself unable to concentrate. I set aside my work, folded my arms across my desk, and rested my head. I couldn't even pray. Besides, I had nothing left to say.

Then in my thoughts, God spoke to me. He said, "Becky, you know this sadness you've been feeling? That's a taste of life without God." And immediately God flooded my spirit with peace.

The Bible describes those who don't know Jesus as being "without hope and without God" (Ephesians 2:12). It also says Jesus is our peace (Ephesians 2:14). The grief of miscarriage gave me a glimpse of the hopelessness and inner turmoil I would experience without Jesus Christ in my life. Because I'd had the hope and peace of Jesus since I was a child, I didn't fully appreciate it until it was hidden from me for a time.

It was like when the fog lifts off the mountains surrounding my Colorado home. Sometimes the morning fog makes it appear as if there are no mountains at all, but eventually the sun burns away the vapor and the mountains reappear. The truth is the mountains never left. I just couldn't see them for a time.

The same was true of my grief. Eventually the clouds passed. The darkness lifted. And I could see the God that had been there the whole time.

'Tis The Reason For The Season

by Sheila Eismann

In the hustle and bustle
 of the season,
Have you stopped
 to consider the reason?

Why do we toil
 so everything will be first rate,
Waiting until December 25th
 just to celebrate?

Is your heart stirred by the good food,
 tree, or gifts,
The music, cards, and parties,
 or the opening of ski-lifts?

Do you long to meet with family and friends
 that you all love so dearly,
To reminisce of times long ago
 that you still remember clearly?

Perhaps the passing of loved ones
 makes you feel lonely and sad,
It's hard to get through this time
 because you're just not very glad.

Millenniums ago, the prophet Isaiah foretold,
 that the virgin would bear a son,
Born in Bethlehem and called Immanuel,
 His advent was a most humble one.

This baby boy, better known as Jesus,
 came to die on the cross for our sin.
Until we repent and accept Him as Savior,
 there's no way we will ever win.

Is Jesus knocking on the door of your heart
    or have you already let Him in?
Are you wearing your robe of righteousness
    or are you still living in your sin?

So take a moment, amidst your frantic pace,
    to commune with the King of Kings.
For no one else can deliver joy and peace;
    none other gives the life He brings!

Understanding Sacrifice

by Jane Freund

Think back to when you were eleven years old. Where were you living? What family members were around you? Did you have a home you knew? What were you concerned about in your life? Keep those thoughts and images in your head as you read this story about George, an eleven-year-old who came to America on December 1, 1938. In his young life, he had experienced more than many adults let alone most children his age.

George's parents had met in his native Austria in the mid 1920s. Hans was an attorney and Gertrude was a bright and engaging young woman who was just starting to find her way in the world. Her parents, Alois and Marie Goldmann, were particularly protective of Trude, their only child. They became more concerned as her relationship with Hans became more serious and marriage was discussed. Trude had been weakened by tuberculosis and had a narrow pelvis which could make having children difficult. But Hans and Trude married anyway and she became pregnant with their first child.

George was born on August 6, 1927 in Vienna, Austria. He was welcomed into the family but sadly one member was soon to leave them. Giving birth proved to be too much for Trude and she died just six weeks after George's birth. Devastated, the Goldmanns cut off contact with their son-in-law.

Hans had family and servants who helped him raise young George, but that too was short-lived. During World War I, Hans had been gassed and was stricken with tuberculosis. Realizing that he did not have much time to live, he reconciled with the Goldmanns and made arrangements for George to go live with his grandparents. Hans died when George was about nine years old. However, he did have his grandparents to raise him and that turned out to be an incredible blessing.

Alois and Marie Goldmann were Jewish and had an amazing presence of mind to realize what Adolph Hitler was doing to the Jewish people. They knew that Austria, Czechoslovakia (where they also had relatives) and Europe in general was not a good place for their young grandson to be. Fortunately, Hans had a sister, brother-in-law and nephew who lived in New York City so arrangements were made for George to go to live with them. The Goldmanns also tried to leave but since they didn't have a sponsor in America like George did, they were not allowed to leave.

But that limitation did not stop the Goldmanns from making what must have been a heart wrenching decision: they sent their only descendant and only flesh-and-blood to America knowing that they would likely never see him again. That instinct turned out to be correct as Alois and Marie Goldmann were murdered at Auschwitz toward the end of World War II.

As a born-again Christian, I try to understand the depth of God's sacrifice of sending His only begotten Son, Jesus Christ, to die for my sins. I do not have children and thus don't necessarily understand that parent-child bond and the associated feelings. So, I look to the Goldmanns to try to wrap my heart and my head around what sacrifice feels and looks like.

I can particularly relate to the Goldmanns because I am related to them. For these amazing people who taught me so much about sacrifice were my great-grandparents and George, their only descendant, was my Dad.

Now I understand sacrifice.

Where is Sanctuary?

by Tina Frederick

I stood at the edge,
The rage, the pain it tears the soul
And leaves me bleeding,
Bleeding like never before.

Staring down into the abyss,
Black, dark total nothingness
And it whispers to me
"Come forget, forget."

Standing on the edge of madness,
Is this real or make believe?
My soul bared for all to see:
Ripped, naked, scarred, and screaming

Laughter in the shadows,
Don't look at me, don't see me like this.
Alone, denying, I'm dying inside
From all the tears I'm crying.

And the pain it's heavy.
Please I don't want to feel it no more.
Help me find what I'm looking for.

And the soul cries out "Where is Sanctuary?"

Short Stories

Haunted

by Giselle Jeffries

Anabeth, whose long light brown hair was pulled back in a ponytail, pulled the truck up to the front of our new home. Suzy, age 6, was looking out the back passenger side window with big, excited eyes. Her nose and hands pressed up against the glass and her long, curly, light brown hair hanging down over her shoulders. Nicky, age 8, with short, spiky, light brown hair, sat in the back behind Anabeth. His arms were crossed and he looked up at the roof of the truck with a look of nonchalance on his face.

Anabeth turned off the ignition and unlocked the doors for the kids to get out. As Suzy and Nicky were still slowly unfastening their seatbelts and getting out of the car, Anabeth came around the front of the truck to open the passenger side door and let me out. I leaped down from the seat and walked over the grass to sniff around for a good spot. The second I relieved myself I realized something was wrong. I looked around, but all I saw was my family, the truck, and the new house.

The house my family bought was a white, two-floor Victorian with a wrap around patio. The paint on the outside walls and the patio was faded; showing the brown wood underneath. There was also a fenced in yard in the back. The wood on the fence was filled with holes and wind damaged, but surprisingly still standing. I guessed the house had to be around a hundred years old and appeared to have been empty for more than fifty years.

The house seemed to tower over us, like a mountain in the dark. The windows appeared like eyes that glared down at us as my family unpacked the moving trailer. The front door stood wide open and an empty coldness leaked out to wrap itself around me. From the house itself I could feel a sort of aura; it was like a bubble around the whole property. I even saw someone from one of the second floor windows or at least a silhouette of a man. He glared at us with hollow, glowing eyes; eyes that could be seen in complete darkness. This strange man also seemed to be sending forth an aura. It felt like he was trying to push us back and keep us from going any farther. I could feel his possessiveness and anger. He expressed a very clear baleful nature. Like the house, he was cold and empty. I knew instantly that this man in the window was not human. This man was a ghost and evil.

I looked back at my family and felt fear go through me. My heart started beating fast and my brain went into overdrive as I saw little Suzy and Nicky run for the house. Suzy was smiling, expressing all her joy of finally getting to beat her brother at something. "I pick first! I pick first!" she yelled as she blew past me. Nicky ran right behind her, claiming boys were supposed to go first.

I leaped forward, passing both children in less than five seconds, and stopped in the doorway; blocking them from getting in. "Stop!" I barked. Suzy halted, but Nicky ignored me and continued running up to the door. "No!" I growled as I leaped on Nicky.

Nicky moved back, almost losing his balance. At first he had a look of surprise on his face, but then it was replaced with irritation. "Stupid dog." Nicky said as he brushed me away and went in.

Suzy stayed frozen in front of me, afraid of what I might do next. I walked forward and brushed my head against her side, assuring her I am only trying to protect them.

She reached down and petted me. As she did so, she told me, "This is our new home, Teddy. It's okay." She grabbed my collar lightly and led me into the house. "Come see my new room."

I followed Suzy into the house, the ghost's aura getting stronger as we began stepping through the entryway. That was when I felt a break in the world around us; the aura I felt coming from the house gripped itself around me like jello and then slid off as we fully entered the house. It was like I stepped into another dimension or something. I felt myself instinctively pull back; wiggling around and trying to drag Suzy out the door with me. Suzy planted her feet on the floor and held on to me. "Teddy… Teddy…" she chanted; her struggle to hold on to me and keep me from running back outside showing in her voice. "Stop Teddy… Stop." But I couldn't stop; we needed to get out. So I continued to resist until Suzy let go and fell to the floor crying. I stopped. I didn't want to be in the house. I didn't want my family in the house. But they didn't understand. I walked up to Suzy, the sensation of the ghost's aura pressing strong against me. I put my nose to her nose and whimpered. I couldn't make them understand, but I could protect them as much as I could until they realized the danger.

Suzy wiped her eyes on her arm, grabbed my collar, and pulled herself up. "It's okay, Teddy." she said as she tugged my collar and led me upstairs. "We'll get used to this place."

The steps creaked from the weight of our bodies, paint pealed from the hand railing, and a shadowy darkness swept over us. Suzy continued to talk to me. She told me about how we were going to make new friends and how she was excited about starting school in a new town, but then her voice faded into the background. I was more focused on the ghost who lived in this house. I wanted to know where he was now and where Nicky walked off to. Then the stairs made a slight turn and entered immediately into a small living room with a window overlooking the front yard. There was a hallway to the left with three bedrooms: two rooms across from each other and the last at the end of the hall. This hallway broke off to the right and lead to a bathroom. Nicky came out of the first door on the right, jerked his thumb over his shoulder and said, "I get this one." A shadow passed behind him and went down the floor and under my paws. I felt it get really cold, like someone suddenly turned the air conditioner on high. I felt my hair stand up on my skin and saw Suzy and Nicky shiver. I pulled back again and whimpered.

"That dog is starting to get weird." Nicky said.

"He's just nervous." Suzy responded. "Come on, Teddy," she said as she led me to the room on the left.

I could tell this room had once been a child's room. The walls were a faded light pink and the ceiling was painted dark blue with white clouds. An empty toy chest sat under the window – one of its locks broken and hanging, its lid wide open. Paint stained the floor by the table and chair that were left standing by the chest.

Suzy walked to the window – still holding onto my collar – and looked out. A tree had grown out there and was blocking most of the view. "I like this room," she said. "What do you think?" I looked up at her and found her looking at me with a smile on her face.

"Suzy, Nicky." Anabeth called from downstairs.

"Up here, Mom." Nicky called from his new room.

I heard the steps creak as Anabeth came up the stairs. "Is Suzy up there with you?"

"Yeah, I'm here."

Suzy and I started heading out of the room just as Anabeth reached the top of the stairs. "I see you two found your rooms."

Nicky was standing in the doorway. He shrugged in response. "You couldn't find a newer house?"

Anabeth sighed as she set the boxes she was carrying down. "You know this is all we can afford. Did you want to stay in that apartment forever?"

Nicky didn't respond.

"I like our new house." Suzy said from my side. "It's much bigger and I get my own room."

"Why don't you two come down and help with the smaller things?"

I stood next to Suzy and watched as she unfolded one of the boxes and pulled out a few Barbies. She walked over to one of the two shelves placed next to the closet and set them in a sitting position on the very top. She came back over to the box and repeated the process until the box was empty and both shelves were filled with Barbies and stuffed animals. Then she went to another box, which was filled with pictures wrapped in newspaper. She carefully unwrapped each one and tacked them on the wall. These were pictures of the family, along with drawings and paintings. While she was tacking up the first picture she pulled out, one of the whole family on a beach, my attention was reverted to the black shadowy figure that came through the doorway. It wasn't like a normal shadow though. Instead of moving along the wall or the floor, it walked right into the room in almost full human form with vague facial expressions. The figure also looked like it was glowing around the edges. I hunched down, my hair stood up all over my body, and I let out a growl. "Stay away."

The ghost didn't listen and continued gliding into the room.

"I'm warning you."

"It's okay, Teddy." Suzy said as she turned around to grab another picture. She took a quick glance around to find what upset me and only saw Nicky as he left his room to head downstairs. "It's only Nicky." Suzy turned back to the wall and continued with aligning the pictures.

While her back was turned, the ghost grabbed her dolls, its arms taking a more solid form as they wrapped around several dolls at once. He glided over to the box and lightly dropped them in. He stopped to look at me and laughed.

I let out a bark that made Suzy jump.

"What's the matter, Teddy?" She said as she turned around and walked over to me. "Do you need to go…" She paused at the boxes, noticing her dolls inside. "I thought I took them all out." She looked at the shelves and saw that one was half full.

I lowered myself onto my stomach and let out a whimper.

"Did you do that?" Suzy asked me.

I stayed lying on the floor, my eyes looking up at her. And although I wasn't look at the ghost, I could feel he was still in the room. He had wandered back toward the bookshelves and was just hovering there, waiting.

"Suzy! Nicky!" Anabeth called from the kitchen. "Pizza's here."

"Pizza!" Suzy cried with joy. "Come on, Teddy."

I ran after Suzy, following her down the stairs and into the entrance hall, through the living room on the left, and into the kitchen on the right. Nicky was already in there and helping himself to three slices of pizza.

"Don't eat all of it." Suzy cried as she jumped into the first seat she reached and grabbed a couple slices for herself.

I walked over to the refrigerator and moved the bowls Anabeth put down for me with my nose so I could have a place to sit and still be able to see my family.

"Why aren't you guys using plates?" Anabeth asked sternly when she turned from the refrigerator with three cans of sprite in her hands and saw Suzy and Nicky using napkins to hold their food.

"You didn't unpack them yet." Nicky responded, pointing at the box under the cabinets.

Anabeth gave a surprised and embarrassed look. "That's odd. I could have sworn I took them all out."

"Don't worry, Mommy." Suzy said. "Same thing happened to me when I was taking my things out."

Anabeth sighed and walked over to the box. She pulled out three plates and placed them on the table. Suzy and Nicky grabbed one and placed their slices on them.

"Maybe it was a ghost." Nicky said. Then he looked at Suzy, wiggled the fingers of his free hand, and said, "Oooo."

"Mommy?" Suzy whimpered, turning her face away from Nicky to give Anabeth a pleading look to make him stop and to make sure he was just joking.

"Don't scare your sister, Nicky. Now Suzy, you know there is no such thing as ghosts."

Nicky smiled and laughed softly to himself. He enjoyed scaring Suzy and it was instances like these that made it so much easier. Every time something strange happened and Suzy was somewhere close by, Nicky would claim it was a ghost or a monster and scare Suzy into crying. At our old apartment, Nicky would hide in Suzy's closet and come out in the middle of the night. Anabeth put a stop to it by checking the closet, looking under the bed, closing Suzy's door, and even making sure Nicky was in his room before going to bed.

Until everything was finally put away and all the boxes were folded up and left in the garage, the moving and disappearing of objects didn't stop. In addition every day that went by only made Suzy's fear worse. To comfort her I started sleeping in the room with her. At first I was on the bed, but after a couple days I moved to the floor to show her no matter how far away I was, I would still be there to protect her. Nicky wasn't any help though. He always found some way to scare her and keep her fear implacable.

On our seventh day in the house, Suzy was on the couch watching Garfield and I was on the floor at her feet. Nicky was in the arm chair near the corner of the room, slouched in like he wanted to hide. I could tell he wasn't paying attention to the TV. His eyes seemed to be focused on the wall and gave off a glassy appearance. Anabeth was in the kitchen cooking lunch. Everyone in the house was quiet and keeping to themselves.

The ghost, however, seemed to have disappeared, but I knew better than to believe that. I never let the ghost slip past my radar. If I couldn't see him lurking in the corner, I could sense where he was in the house. For example, I could tell he was in the living room upstairs because of the strength of his aura in that particular area of the house. I also learned to focus my hearing and to feel the difference in the auras he sent out. When he was being territorial and inpatient, he would attempt to strangle my family with his menacing aura. Luckily I was the only one who could feel it and this failure upset him. When he was plotting his next move, his aura would just float in the air like a mark on the territory.

Although my attention was on the ghost in the back of the room, I saw from the corner of my eye Nicky get up and head upstairs with a smile on his face. I figured he had a plan, one that was only going to get him into trouble again. I listened to him as he walked out of the living room, went into the entrance, made the sharp turn up the stairs, and then walked the few feet to his room. It was quiet for another five minutes. I took this time to think about what the ghost was planning and what I would be able to do. If my family was hurt, I would be responsible because I was unable to protect them. That was my job as a dog; I had to protect my family and love them no matter what. Then I realized if anything did happen, it would be because I wasn't paying attention, so I stopped thinking and started paying attention to where the ghost was. Just as I expected, I was caught off my guard. The ghost had made his way downstairs and was now hovering in the corner behind us. Luckily, he hadn't made his move yet. Still, I couldn't let my mind wander again, because next time….

"BWAAAHHAHAHAHA!"

I jumped right up onto my feet. Suzy tripped over me as she tried to escape, and something shattered on the kitchen floor. I quickly regained my balance and turned to face the ghost, but it was just Nicky, who was now laughing uncontrollably from behind the couch. He grabbed his stomach with both hands and fell to his knees. I could see his face starting to turn purple from the lack of air. I also heard the ghost laughing from where he stood at the back of the room. I turned back around to face Suzy, who was wrapped in a ball on the floor and crying.

"What the hell is the matter with you?" yelled Anabeth as she came storming into the living room. "I told you a dozen times already to stop scaring your sister!" She grabbed Nicky by the arm and started hauling him through the house and up the upstairs. "You also made me break one of my best plates! So for the rest of the day you are going to be in your room! No TV! No video games! No lunch! You can come back down only after you thought of what you did and can truly say sorry and can promise to never do it again!" Then she slammed the door closed and came back downstairs.

I was sitting beside Suzy and licking her face. I wanted her to know it was okay and that I would never let anyone hurt her. She didn't move though. She stayed curled up in a little ball and continued crying. Anabeth entered the room and knelt down beside me so she could pick Suzy up. I followed her as she carried Suzy in her arms, her muscles straining to hold her. She set Suzy down at the table and went to the freezer, turning her back only for a second so she could get Suzy some ice cream. She placed the small container in front of Suzy and hugged her.

"Don't cry, Suzy." Anabeth said while still hugging her. "It's okay. There is no such thing as ghosts."

Suzy sniffed and nodded, but the tears never stopped. Anabeth kissed Suzy on the cheek and went to clean up the mess and finish preparing the food.

* * *

The night seemed to drag on forever. I was lying on the floor at the foot of Suzy's bed for what seemed like hours; just waiting for the ghost to attack, but he only floated up and down the hallway with his aura gathered around himself. It was like he was trying to hide from me, but he only managed to make it a whole lot easier for me to know exactly where he was in the house – right to the very spot. He did, however, manage to make me very impatient. I tried to relax and convince myself that I would be ready when he made his first attack, but all I wanted to do was jump up and run after him. I wanted to rip him apart. I didn't want to wait for whatever he had planned. The waiting made me feel like I was about to explode; it was so excruciating.

It had to have been four hours before I felt the ghost release his hold on his aura. I felt it sweep under Suzy's door and fill the room. I lifted up my head and saw him glide through the doorway, his shadowy, glowing figure showing through the darkness. I felt my heart pound against my ribs and I instinctively jumped up off the floor and onto the bed. I laid my whole body over Suzy. This was it. The ghost was ready to attack. I could feel it in the air which had gotten really cold. I could also feel it in his aura which had wrapped around Suzy and me. It was pulling tight, like a rope, but the way Suzy was sleeping I could tell I was still the only one feeling it. The ghost didn't come to the bed though. Instead he turned and went to the bookshelves. I glared at him, wondering what his plan was. It seemed like minutes had gone by before I saw him grab the edge of the bookshelf and give it a shake, causing a few dolls to fall off. I looked at Suzy, but thankfully she was still sleeping. Then he moved along the wall – slowly. He was just gliding along the wall, like he was trying to lure me away like a cat after a laser light. I didn't move. A picture frame fell, then another, and then another. It was after the fifth picture that Suzy woke up.

"What was that?" she whispered as she tried to sit up. I saw her eyes move to her dolls, which she had carefully put away, and heard her whimper.

I licked her face, but didn't move off of her.

The shadow moved along the wall and stopped at the table. I saw its ghostly hand wrap around the lamp and I watched as he slowly lifted it up like a weight. It seemed like he had never done this before, wasn't sure what he could do. The lamp floated there for awhile, almost like it was in thin air. I could hear Suzy's heart beating like a team of runners on a racetrack and her breathing stop in fear as she noticed what I was looking at. Then the lamp soared across the room. Suzy wrapped her arms around me and let out a scream as the lamp shattered against the wall above us, the shards raining down. Then a light from somewhere in the hall came on shining its away under the door. There were two sets of feet flying across the floor. Nicky got to the room first and then Anabeth.

"Suzy, what's wrong?" Anabeth asked as she ran past a frozen Nicky in the doorway to grab Suzy up in her arms. It wasn't until she got to the bed that she noticed the broken lamp shards scattered across the pillow and in Suzy's hair. Suzy's grip on me was tight and her face was buried in my golden hair. It took awhile, but Anabeth broke Suzy's grip and pulled her up from under me and hugged her against her chest.

"There's a ghost in my room!" Suzy cried from Anabeth's arms.

"There is no such thing as ghosts, Suzy. Nicky just made that up to scare you."

"B-but th-the lamp, i-it f-flew a-across t-the room."

Anabeth didn't respond; she only hugged Suzy closer and glared at Nicky.

"Don't look at me." Nicky said, after realizing he was being stared at. "I was asleep. You even saw me come in here."

Anabeth got up, still holding a crying Suzy in her arms, and glanced around the room with a thoughtful, yet scared, look on her face. "We're all sleeping in my room until we can call someone to look at the house."

"You need to call ghost busters." Nicky said.

Anabeth paused halfway to the door. She didn't say anything. She only looked at him with a terrified look on her face. Then she walked out of the room. Nicky and I followed.

* * *

Suzy and Nicky fell back asleep on Anabeth's bed. Suzy was snuggled up against Anabeth; Nicky was a few inches away, determined not to touch them as he slept; and I was on the floor at the foot of the bed. All the lights in the room, including the bathroom light, were on as a form of comfort to them as they all fell back asleep. I, however, didn't expect the ghost to stop even for a moment. I had the feeling the first attack was just a warning, a preparation for whatever he had planned next. He wanted us to be afraid. He wanted us to try and escape so he could come after us like a wolf and his prey, but I wasn't going to give him that satisfaction. I was going to get my family out of this house, but first they needed to sleep so they could be ready to move.

I continued to stay awake and focus on the ghost who was still in Suzy's room. His aura was now emanating throughout the entire house and was wrapped around my family. The ghost didn't seem to be moving though, which made me believe he was waiting for something to happen first.

I heard Nicky sit up and slide out of bed and head for the bathroom. That was when the ghost moved out of the room and started gliding through the wall between Suzy's room and Anabeth's. I watched as the ghost came into the room, just a fog in the bright lights. Then Nicky came out and headed out of the room. The ghost followed and so did I. I didn't want to leave the other two alone, but Nicky seemed the most vulnerable at the moment. Maybe that was the ghost's plan, to attack us individually. The ghost followed right behind Nicky, with me on their tail pretending to just be tagging along.

"What do you want?" Nicky asked just before he opened the refrigerator. He pulled out an orange juice and poured it into the glass he always left by the refrigerator for easy access. "Shoo," he said, waving his free hand. "Go back upstairs."

I just sat down by the table and looked up at him, tilting my head to the side and lifting up my ears.

The ghost hovered next to him and I wasn't sure what to do about it. It never just hovered by anyone before. Then it reached out a hand. "No!" I barked. I was now standing back up.

Nicky jumped, startled by my out of the blue bark. "You stupid dog." he said as he set the glass back down and headed out of the kitchen. The ghost didn't pull back. He moved just as Nicky moved, turning into a puff of smoke just before gliding into him.

Nicky came to a sudden stop. For a moment he just stood there, which made me nervous. I could feel all the hairs on my body stand up and a shiver ran through me. Nicky slowly lifted his hands and began examining each individual movement he made. First he took one hand and extended it out in front of him. He moved each finger individually. He slowly turned his head and glared down at me. The eyes that used to be brown were now two hollow black voids. He made, with some struggle, a sinister smile.

I lowered my head and growled a deep throated, "Get out of him."

The ghost chuckled. It sounded weird coming from Nicky's body. It sounded so abstract. Just then all the drawers and cabinets in the kitchen flew open, startling me. Some of the drawer fell to the floor, scattering silverware all over the place and a knife flew into Nicky's hand.

I threw myself at him. I had no choice. I even tried not to think about the fact that it was still Nicky's body. I had to convince myself it wasn't Nicky anymore. But it still hurt me to do what I was doing. I knocked him down, causing him to hit the ground hard. I grabbed his shirt in my teeth and started ripping as I growled for the ghost to get out of him. Saliva pooled out of my mouth, my hair was raised on end, and my nails were extended.

The sound of feet flying down the stairs came to my ears and I realized our commotion woke Anabeth and Suzy. I stopped the ripping, but not the growling, just as Anabeth came into the kitchen.

"Nicky!" Anabeth screamed as she tried to pull me off of him. "Get off him!"

A shooting pain shot through my side and I let out a whine as I pulled away from Nicky and fell into Anabeth. Nicky jumped up, finally free of my weight, and lunged at us with the knife still in his hand. I leap back up and went straight for the knife this time. I gripped Nicky's wrist in my mouth, trying not to bit too hard, and tried to get him to let go. His free hand grabbed my collar and a deep voiced scream came from his mouth, but he still didn't let go of the knife. I knew this wasn't going to work the way I was doing it, so what I did next made me feel horrible. I bit down. My teeth broke through his skin and blood poured out into my mouth and stained my golden hair. The ghost let out an even louder scream; a horrible, unworldly scream that echoed through the house as he tried to pull his arm away, his other hand still yanking on my collar. I heard and felt bones crack between my teeth as well as the sound of the knife hitting the linoleum floor. Nicky fell to his knees just as I let go. I took that second of vulnerability and jumped on him, knocking him on his backwards..

"Noooo!" Anabeth yelled. As she ran over to us.

I saw the ghost leave Nicky's body, soar to the ceiling and seep through. I thought of Suzy all alone in Anabeth's room and panicked. I leaped off of Nicky, leaving him in Anabeth's care, and ran upstairs to get Suzy. The time it took to leave the kitchen, run through the living room, reach the entrance, and make the sharp turn to run up the stairs felt like an eternity. It was like being in a dream where I am trying to get somewhere in a hurry but gravity seems to be pulling me back and slowing me down. My heart pounded with fear and my brain raced with the possibilities of what I might find as I finally reached to next floor and ran down the hall for Anabeth's room. Luckily I found Suzy hiding under the bed, trying to hold back her crying. I stuck my nose under, licked her face, and whimpered. She crawled out and hugged me around the neck. I tugged, trying to indicate that I wanted her to come with me, but she didn't seem to notice. Her hug loosened as she went to rub her face in my hair, which allowed me to weasel my way out of her grip so I could grab her clothes in my mouth. She seemed to understand. She stood up, grabbed my collar, and followed me out of the room and back downstairs where we found the door wide open and Anabeth outside with Nicky, unconscious in her arms.

"Mommy!" Suzy yelled. She let go of my collar and ran for Anabeth just as we cleared the doorway, the houses aura wrapping around me and sliding off, allowing us to enter back into our dimension - and the door slammed itself shut behind me.

The Savior of Poplar Grove

by Benita Nelson

Ethel Chase had shopped at the same supermarket for the past 41 years. The Super Val-u-Mart had weathered floods, down-economies, labor strikes, and competition from national chains that preyed upon the local merchant like a 20-year old, gold digger preys upon an ailing 90-year old, oil tycoon. Through it all Ethel had remained loyal and despite the chain stores' promises to stretch a shopper's dollar until it snapped, she seldom shopped anywhere else. And why would she? For her the Super Val-u-Mart was ideally located; only four blocks from home. Setting out by automobile, Ethel's safe arrival was virtually guaranteed through a series of right-hand-only turns the entirety of her round trip. With her encroaching cataracts, left-hand turns across traffic were an invitation for disaster.

The Super Val-u-Mart was dependable, predictable, comfortable. The produce department hadn't moved in twenty years. Every Wednesday was double-coupon day—a godsend for those on tight budgets—and she could find the Lorna Doones simply by counting the paces from the front door. Forty-eight until recently. Now it was fifty-seven; the aluminum walker had slowed her down considerably.

She hadn't grown up in the neighborhood but she had grown old in it. Poplar Grove was one of those tract home developments built in the sixties that had sprung up in booming areas like spring weeds invading an un-tended garden. Homogenous homes of six different floor plans all with white rain gutters, composite roofs, and single-car garages had been cranked out in metered fashion like blocks of extruded Play-Doh. Strip malls that offered dry cleaners, teriyaki joints, sub sandwich shops, take-and-bake pizza places, and French nail salons had erupted around the periphery. Poplar Grove had it all.

But Poplar Grove was no longer a shiny jewel of Pax Americana. No, not by a long shot. When Ethel Chase and her family had first moved in, it had been a neighborhood where kids rode bicycles with banana seats, fathers manned barbecue grills at cookouts, and mothers baked cupcakes and popcorn balls for the PTA bake sale—in dresses. Every backyard had a Slip N Slide, every driveway a Buick.

Over the years as the middle class traded-up for homes on larger lots with professional landscaping and fancy security gates, the neighborhood evolved from the apex of the middle-class American Dream to one of lower-end starter homes ripe for takeover by the less affluent. Eventually the neighborhood degraded into rental properties and flophouses crammed with refugees and immigrant workers. With average tenants unable to secure 30-year financing, Poplar Grove eventually fell to the criminal element. The land of enchantment was now dominated by crack houses and meth labs. Mayberry had literally gone to pot.

It was Tuesday morning and Ethel was short on pantry staples. She could not wait 24 hours for double-coupon day. She needed milk, had used her last roll of paper towels to wipe a prune juice spill, and was precariously low on Lorna Doones. As she had no coupons for any of her necessities, she easily found more than one reason to justify this morning's extra trip to the supermarket.

Ethel collected her things, pulled on her Isotoner gloves, slipped into her lavender-colored, knee-length, wool coat—it was quite a chilly morning—cinched it tight, and headed out to the Super Val-u-Mart in her eighteen year-old Buick Century.

As he had done for the past eight years, Darnell Watson, Super Val-u-Mart's dayshift security guard, greeted Ethel Chase at the store's main entrance. "G'mornin' Miz Chase. You lookin' 'specially lovely today, Ma'am," he remarked as he tipped his blue hat to her. A gold front tooth twinkled like rapper's bling as the morning sun landed upon his smile.

Although many years past hot flashes, Ethel felt her face flush as she waved off Darnell's complimentary affections. "Oh stop it, Darnell. I'm an old woman and I know cotton-pickin' well I'm nowhere near *lovely* anymore." Still, she smiled, clearly enjoying the flirtatious, albeit harmless, attention. After all, Darnell was a strong and firm man of twenty-eight. Though she didn't favor his dark skin, Ethel could certainly appreciate the fine physical specimen that was Darnell Watson, even at her advanced age.

Besides his physical appeal, Darnell was a fine human being. He'd moved into the neighborhood fifteen years ago with his mama and seven siblings, Darnell being the only decent one of the bunch. Two of his brothers had been murdered while engaging in gang activities, two more were in prison, and God only knew what had become of his sisters-turned-crack whores. All Ethel knew was that their offspring of all ages and sizes, deposited there to be raised by their grandmother, ran around their granny's front yard like a pack of wild dogs.

With two years of community college under his belt, Darnell had married his high school sweetheart and the couple had two children whom he loved and supported. There was no way Darnell was going to repeat the mistakes of his parents and siblings. He knew exactly how to achieve the American Dream and he was going after it with all he had.

As Darnell ushered Ethel into the store he caught a glimpse of fresh graffiti on the storefront and grimaced. Gang markings by an affiliate of the West Poplar Kings. A tag by gang member, Loco Duke, a punk who lived three houses down from his. Darnell knew that as soon as the graffiti was cleaned off, new murals would appear in their place. He was not pleased.

He also wasn't pleased that his neighborhood had become so dangerous, so corrupt that the supermarket had had to install a metal detector at the main entrance. But he accepted it knowing it was for the best, while saddened and disheartened that the world, his neighborhood, his home, had come to this.

BEEP! BEEP! BEEP! BEEP! As it had done every time Ethel entered the store since the metal detector had been installed, her walker set off the alarm. Although she had braced herself for the inevitable barrage of warning sirens, she still startled and flinched. And as he had done every time since Ethel first triggered the alarm, Darnell waved her through and killed the siren.

"Sorry 'bout that nasty ol' alarm, Miz Chase. You go on through now, ya hear?"

Ethel patted her chest to calm her nerves, smiled, and replied, "I never get used to that thing, Darnell. I must look like an old fool to you."

"No, no, course not Miz Chase. I'm sorry for that thing, but you know it's for the best."

Ethel nodded. "I know." She pointed out the front door at the graffiti and shook her head, clearly disgusted. "I see the local lowlifes are up to their old tricks."

Darnell smiled. "Punks. We'll get it cleaned up."

"Won't stop them though, will it?"

Darnell shook his head. "Afraid not, Miz Chase. 'Fraid not."

Ethel shuffled toward the grocery cart corral while clinging to her walker to steady her feeble gait. Darnell called out to her, "Unadvertised special on pork loin today, Miz Chase. Best hurry, though." Darnell sniffed at the air circulating from the bakery in back and fought off his craving for a jelly doughnut. He wouldn't dream of leaving his post for such a frivolous indulgence.

Olivia Newton-John's *Hopelessly Devoted to You* played through the store's sound system. It was a sickly sweet tune that Ethel feared would stick in her head for the rest of the day. An earworm they call it. Or at least that's what she'd read somewhere. She waved at Darnell without looking back. "Thank you kindly, Darnell." She steadied herself by grabbing a cart handle then neatly folded her walker and placed it, along with her two re-usable shopping bags, in the basket. And off she went.

Jamal "JJ Chilli Rage" Grant sat behind the wheel of his harshly-used, late-nineties model, Mitsubishi Eclipse, chewing on a toothpick while watching the old woman shuffle into the Super Val-u-Mart. "Piece of cake," he said to himself. He flicked the toothpick out the window and was about to get out of the car when he paused to check his watch.

The armored truck wasn't due for another twenty minutes, but still he wanted to get in and get out. Get it done. Get his haul of cash before the armored truck drivers packing shotguns and pistols rolled in and rolled out, making off with his take, all in less than two minutes. Cash gone.

Jamal took a breath and held back remembering what his boss had told him. "Be patient," his boss had said. "Wait for just the right moment.

Be expedient, but don't get in too much of a rush. That's when mistakes are made."

Last night there had been one winner in the MegaCash lottery drawing, the largest cash pot in seven years. Three hundred and seventy million dollars. Or thereabouts. Greedy, jackpot-hungry gamblers from every corner of society wanted a piece of it—wanted all of it. And most of them paid for their tickets in cash. Greenbacks. Dead presidents. Cash that filled the Super Val-u-Mart's safe to the brim. Cash that still had not been picked up. Cash that would be his in a few minutes.

Technically speaking, Jamal was at work, on assignment from his boss. And technically-speaking, Jamal was going to make sure he kept all the cash—every last dollar. His boss, whom he called Ol' Whitey, had given him strict orders. "The morning after someone finally wins the big jackpot, enter the Super Val-u-Mart unarmed, between nine and nine-ten a.m. Get a shopping cart. Head straight for the paper towels. A gun will be stashed behind a pack of Burly paper towels. Grab a pack of towels and put them in the cart, using them to hide the gun. Return to the front of the store and shoot out the surveillance cameras above the check stands. They're high overhead—four of them—just like those black bulbs that look like Martian eyeballs in the casinos. After—and only *after*—you've shot out the cameras, take out the security guard—he'll be armed so be ready. Then go straight for the cash in the office. Any customers or bagboys get in your way, take 'em out. As soon as you have the cash, get the hell outta there."

JJ Chilli Rage gazed out his side window to appreciate the fresh artwork, courtesy of Loco Duke, on the front of the supermarket. Markings from his old gang. Markings that made him wistful for the days of running with the boys from the block. He shook his head and laughed a little. He missed Loco Duke. But this was business. He'd left the West Poplar Kings—making him a marked traitor—for a better-paying employer, Ol' Whitey. The jobs were fewer but the payoffs were bigger and the plans more thoroughly vetted. While many of his former gang members were dead or doing time, Jamal was alive and free. To a point, anyway.

He looked at his watch one more time. It was time.

Jamal got out of the car and walked through the store's main entrance, making a point of pulling a slip of paper that looked like a shopping list from his front pants pocket. Ol' Whitey had told him to enter the store as if he was there simply to pick up a few necessities, not to rob them blind. Jamal looked up briefly to make eye contact with the security guard, Darnell, an acquaintance from the neighborhood. Jamal's quick study of Darnell confirmed that the security guard was armed with a handgun that appeared about as menacing as a toy starter pistol. Stupid. Weak. "Piece of cake," Jamal thought to himself. Again.

Darnell recognized JJ Chilli Rage and half expected him to set off the metal detector. But he didn't, which was all part of Ol' Whitey's plan. That's what separated Ol' Whitey from the leaders of the West Poplar Kings, who would have stormed in with guns held sideways, blasting everything in their path, scaring kittens, children, and anything else within a block of the store, the authorities alerted before the gang even hit the front door. And when all was said and done, at least half their crew would have either been captured or killed.

Jamal nodded at Darnell. With no exchange of words, thumbs hooked into the waistband of his pants, Darnell nodded back, his eyes intentionally locked on Jamal to make the punk self-conscious. Jamal knew that the basic assumption was, once in a gang, always a gang-banger. And it was partly true; one could never really leave the gang life. If the law didn't catch up with you, the old gang did. He knew Darnell knew it, too. He also knew Darnell was judging him and his score wasn't good.

Jamal recognized *Hopelessly Devoted to You* seeping from the sound system. Music white people liked. *Old* white people. He quickly scanned the store. One check stand was open with two customers in line—both women and both purchasing large pink bakery boxes marred with thumbprint-sized grease stains. Probably doughnuts. Probably for meetings later in the day. He hadn't noticed the scent of fresh-baked pastries wafting about the store before he'd seen the pink bakery boxes. His mouth watered for an apple fritter. A bony middle-aged man ran the check stand while an equally bony teenage boy stood slack-jawed, ready to bag groceries. Jamal knew he could knock them both cold simply by spitting on them. Piece of cake.

A young woman who doggedly drove an overloaded cart muttered to herself and referred to her shopping list often. A tiny pigtailed girl pushing a miniature shopping cart brought up the rear. The tot lagged several cart-lengths behind her mother, distracted by the purple plush toy in her basket. The pair rounded the corner from the coffee and tea aisle and headed for frozen foods, unaware of anything but the frozen peas and concentrated fruit juices that surrounded them. One man, a Caucasian vagrant, purchased a pack of cigarettes at the customer service counter. Camels. He left the store.

After completing a casual surveillance sweep of the aisles within view, Jamal saw no one else. Tuesday at nine o'clock in the morning was indeed a sleepy hour at the Poplar Grove Super Val-u-Mart.

Jamal looked behind him. The small office with one-way windows was adjacent to the customer service counter, its door slightly ajar. According to his boss, that's where the money was stashed.

As he sauntered toward the shopping cart corral, Jamal felt Darnell's eyes fall away. Surreptitiously, he glanced upward, his eyeballs pierced by the yellowish, abrasive neon lights. The ceiling was high; extraordinarily so. Jamal had been in the grocery store countless times, but had never noticed the extreme ceiling height. It caught him by surprise and made him feel as if he'd never been there before. When he spotted the black, bulbous protrusions from the ceiling, the eyes-in-the-sky as Ol' Whitey had called them, he realized the four targets were further away than he'd anticipated. Hitting each of them on the first shot would be difficult, but not an impossible task. He pulled a cart from the queue and set out toward the paper goods aisle, Burly paper towels the first—and only—item on his list.

Though it was difficult, Ethel Chase ignored the enticing aromas coming from the bakery as she browsed the paper towel section for deals. Her preferred doughnut was the old fashioned and her preferred brand of paper towel was Burly, mostly because of the handsome lumberjack on the packaging although the product was truly of admirable quality. Silly she knew, but as an old woman she was entitled to her secret, if not absurd, fantasies. Alas, Shiny-White towels were on sale while Burly's were not, so Ethel pulled a two-pack from the shelf and tossed it in the cart. Her lumberjack would have to wait until a coupon came in the weekly circular. Ethel's next stop was the dairy case along the back wall and then off to juice aisle where she hoped to find yet another unadvertised sale, this time for prune juice.

Jamal's shopping cart had a squeaky wheel, as if he didn't already feel ridiculous enough pushing a cart like some little old lady. He prayed he wouldn't run into anyone he knew.

He checked his watch, Three minutes had passed since he last looked, still plenty of time before the armored car arrived. And yet, Jamal's stomach tumbled. Something could go wrong. So far all of Ol' Whitey's plans had worked like clockwork, but as they say, there's a first time for everything. Even Ol' Whitey's got to be wrong once in a while. He hoped it wasn't this time.

As Ethel neared the end-cap she heard a squeaky wheel; some unfortunate soul had selected a cart with a defective wheel. She looked over her shoulder to see who it was and when she saw the black youth with his untied Adidas, sloppy pants, oversized basketball jersey, and Oakland Raiders cap cocked to the left; she waxed disgusted and hastened her pace. No, this was not like the old days. The neighborhood where she had raised her family was now a much scarier place.

Jamal noticed the old woman speed off after seeing him. "That's right, you go 'head 'n run, old woman. Go 'head 'n run." he muttered to himself. And then he carried out his orders.

After locating the Burly paper towels with their iconic, tall, white male on the package fronts, he pulled the first multi-pack he came to off the shelf. But there was no gun.

He returned it to the shelf and then moved to an identical package to the right. And there it was, just sitting there: a Glock 17 with a fully-loaded thirty-three round magazine. A nice piece indeed. Ol' Whitey did everything right - always.

Ethel Chase sped off, as fast as an old woman with a bad hip and gout can. She wanted to acquire her prune juice, milk, and Lorna Doones quickly. She didn't like the looks of the gang-banger in the paper goods aisle with his mangy, unsophisticated clothing and undereducated demeanor. The less opportunity she had to cross paths with him the better. She'd play it by ear whether or not to take advantage of the pork loin special.

Olivia Newton-John still sapped on and on with *Hopelessly Devoted to You.* Ethel sighed and wished for the song to end.

After placing a quart of 2% in her cart, Ethel set out to find her prune juice. She shuffled up the aisle and after having passed myriad cranberry juice blends, grape juices, and finally V8 in bottles and six-packs, she approached the underappreciated and much maligned prune juice. Just as she placed a 32-ounce bottle of Sunsweet in her cart, a shot rang out. *POP!*

With a jump Ethel looked in the direction of the shot in time to see exploding black plastic bits raining down over the check stands. *POP! POP! POP!* Three more shots rang out, flurries of black plastic jettisoned about the room as the checker and bagboy ran for their lives out the front entrance. "Heeelp!! Run!!" yelled the checker.

"Shoot 'em, Darnell! Shoot 'em!" screamed the bagboy as his gangly legs tore out the main entrance.

A door slammed in the back. Bakery employees making their escape.

The little girl with the miniature cart fell to the floor and covered her ears as she bawled and wailed. "MomMEEE!" Her mother scooped her up and carried her through the front door to the parking lot to safe harbor, abandoning their groceries and purple stuffed animal.

Ethel hastened her gimpy pace and set a course to the front of the store. When she arrived, the only people remaining were Darnell, the store manager whose name was Ted, and the gangbanger. Darnell's gun was aimed straight at the black kid, whose gun was trained on Darnell. The store manager stood a few paces to Darnell's left, his body rigid and hands held high.

Darnell said, "Put the gun down! Put it down NOW! We can work this out!"

With every eye-in-the-sky obliterated, Jamal's attention was focused squarely on Darnell's gun. It did not deter him. He moved quickly toward the pair of store employees, then gestured with his gun to the office. "Gimmee the money! ALL of it!"

Ethel came up behind Jamal. Darnell hollered, "Get back, Miz Chase! Go on, now!"

Ethel ignored him. Jamal glanced over his shoulder but didn't acknowledge her.

Pit stains spread under the arms of the store manager's yellow, short-sleeved shirt like water spilled on a table top. Near tears, he shuddered and spoke up. "We don't have any cash—the armored truck picked it up a few minutes ago."

"Don'chyou lie to me! I know he don't come for fifteen more minutes!" said Jamal. He glanced over his shoulder again at the old woman.

"You heard him, Ted," said Ethel, looking at the store manager. "Give the boy the money. No amount is worth your life."

With his arms still high and hands shaking, the store manager stepped softly toward the little office with the door ajar. He nudged the door until it was wide open, then crouched down and began twirling the combination lock. *Ticka-ticka-ticka-tick.*

"Nothin' funny, Pit Stain." barked Jamal. "Jus' hurry 'n git the cash. No pretendin' you screwed up the combo, cuz you can still open the safe with a bullet in yer damn knee!"

"Urg…" Ted sounded as if he was about to vomit. But he didn't and the final tumbler fell into place, releasing the door and revealing the money.

"Dat's what I'm talkin' 'bout." said Jamal, enamored with the thrill of found treasure. "Okay Pit Stain…bring out da bag and toss it over."

Ethel said, "You're doing fine, Ted. Just toss it on the floor at the boy's feet. *Gently*, dear."

Darnell said to Ethel, "Step back, Miz Chase! Let me handle this, ma'am. I know what I'm doing."

But Ethel stood firm. She knew what had to be done. She said to Jamal, "Get on with it, boy—shoot the guard. And make sure it's a kill shot."

A puzzled and appalled look swept onto Darnell's face. "Miz Chase?" Perplexed, or perhaps disappointed, his shoulders slumped a fraction…just enough for Ethel to notice. But not enough to warn Darnell's defenses. His confusion would be his ultimate traitor.

Jamal couldn't help himself. He simply had to turn the gun sideways. Holding a gun any other way was sissy. *POP! POP!*

Darnell launched backward and fell to the floor as if he'd been dropped by an invisible kick-boxer. He hadn't even tried to catch his fall. *Thunk.* His gun landed on the floor behind him. Cla-*chink.* His left foot twitched. Then, nothing.

You can imagine how the store manager reacted. Yes, he went for

Darnell's gun.

POP! POP!

Jamal shot him in the back. The store manager slumped to the floor, his face planted in the white-speckled linoleum, the gun mere inches from his reach.

Now to finish off the old woman. Still holding the gun at arm's length, Jamal spun to his right, looking forward to blasting the old woman in the face. To finally be free of her. But Ol' Whitey had a surprise for him. A 10-gauge surprise. And Jamal, "JJ Chilli Rage," his eyes wide with shock, undergoing the same confusion that had plagued Darnell only seconds ago, didn't even try to hide his surprise. He couldn't. There was no time.

Ethel cocked the sawed-off shotgun that she'd hidden underneath her coat—right alongside the Glock 17 she'd brought into the Super Val-u-Mart that Jamal now leveled at her—and said, "I told you to never hold a gun like that. It's very unprofessional."

Jamal was frozen, scared stiff of Ol' Whitey. "B-b-but boss…I, I thought—"

"Don't stutter, boy." And then Ethel pulled the trigger.

In one acrid puff, Jamal's face was gone, right along with his pathetic life. Dead before he even hit the floor. Piece of cake.

Ethel threw the shotgun on Jamal's chest. She barely had time to stuff the money from the safe into her re-usable shopping bag before screaming sirens coursed into earshot. The cops. They were coming. Fast. Ethel placed the paper towels into the bag to hide the money, then put the prune juice and milk in the other bag before gathering her walker and heading for the main door. Her Lorna Doones would have to wait until tomorrow.

She loaded her bags and walker into the car and sped off. First she'd drop off her take at home and then would drive to the 'hood for a face-to-face with her new employee, her freshest recruit. JJ Chilli Rage's replacement. Yes, Loco Duke would have to be disciplined. It was far too soon for him to tag his—Ethel's—territory before he'd even executed his first job for her.

Ethel sighed and shook her head in disgust. She'd told JJ Chilli Rage how important timing was. To be patient. To not jump the gun, so to speak. And because he hadn't listened, Ethel wasn't able to get her Lorna Doones.

"*Tsk*. The neighborhood just isn't what it used to be." she muttered.

Cooking Creativity

Comfort Meal Package

by Sheila Eismann

This is a quick, easy and affordable "comfort meal package" that you can take to a family who is celebrating the birth of a new little one, to say "thank you", or to express your sympathy following the death of a loved one. It includes an entrée, salad, rolls, and dessert which are sure to satisfy everyone's food category!

Busy Day Casserole

1 lb ground beef
1 ½ tsp. Worcestershire Sauce
Pepper, salt, garlic salt & dehydrated onion flakes
1 can cut green beans, drained
1 can Cream of Mushroom soup
Tater Tots

Break up the uncooked beef into small pieces and place in the bottom of a disposable aluminum 8 inch square casserole baking dish. Sprinkle uncooked beef with pepper, salt, garlic salt & onion flakes. Drain the green beans and place on top of uncooked beef and seasonings. Spread soup over top of green beans. Finish with a layer of tater tots on top. Recipe is to be baked for 1 hour @ 350 degrees.

(The nice thing about this dish is that it can be frozen and used at a later date if the family should have a lot of food that is delivered to their home simultaneously).

Serve casserole along with a bag of salad greens, a bottle of salad dressing, a tube of refrigerated dinner rolls, butter & jam.

Jell-O Cake

1 white cake mix, any brand
1 small package Jell-O, any flavor
2 small packages instant pudding, any flavor
1 8 oz. container Cool Whip
1 ½ cups milk

Bake cake using directions on package. About 3 minutes before the cake is finished baking, dissolve Jell-O using ¾ cup boiling water and ½ cup cold water. As soon as the cake comes out of the oven and is fully baked, take a large fork and poke holes all over the cake while it is still hot. Pour the liquid Jell-O mixture over the cake. Place cake in refrigerator to cool.

Mix together the 2 small packages of pudding, cool whip and milk and stir until smooth. Spread over cake and place in refrigerator at least one hour before serving.

Enjoy!!

Cook Up Creativity

by Conda V .Douglas

Why does cooking create creativity? Simple. Cooking is creative. One creative behavior leads to more creative behaviors. I've noticed that cooking and baking often free my mind and spirit to renew and roam and when I return to my creative endeavors, it's with a lot more ideas.

For example, my dad was an artist and adored making fudge. He never ate sweets, but every couple of months he'd make an enormous vast amount of fudge, two to four pounds of the sweet stuff. He'd use all the best ingredients and spend hours creating pan after pan. When it had cooled, he'd take a tiny square to taste and make sure it worked. The rest of us ate the rest. I've wondered about why he made fudge and have come to the conclusion that he enjoyed the process. He enjoyed using myriad ingredients, sometimes in new and different ways. And when those new and different ingredients and ways didn't work, he'd toss the batch out and start over (even if we wanted to eat the experiment). Because it was only fudge, only took a limited amount of time, and unlike his art work was not going to go up for sale, he played while he created.

This is transferable to our creative work. When I remember during process to play, to try new ingredients and new ways, and to be willing to toss the entire batch out, I'm much more creative. I'm more likely to get into the flow of the work, instead of slogging through page after page.

I wish I had my dad's fudge recipes, but they were all in his head. Instead in honor of the big food festival, I have included the following which are my favorite recipes. They are easy, almost fool proof, mouthwatering delicious, and guaranteed to get those creative juices flowing too.

English is one of the most difficult languages to learn. One of the problems with English is all the imprecise names. Of which this recipe is an example. This is a recipe for Popovers, which is a misnomer as they don't pop over. This has also been called a Yorkshire Pudding recipe and for this Idaho gal, they're not pudding either. They're low fat rolls and quite tasty for being low fat.

POPOVERS

1 cup fat-free milk or soy milk
1 cup all-purpose (plain) flour (can use unbleached flour)
1/4 tsp salt
4 egg whites or egg substitute 1/2 cup

Preheat the oven to 425 F. Generously coat 6 large metal or glass muffin molds with cooking spray. Heat the muffin molds in the oven for 2 minutes.

In a large bowl, add the milk, flour, salt and egg whites. Using an electric mixer, beat until smooth. Fill the heated muffin molds 2/3 full. Bake in the top part of the oven until golden brown and puffy, about 30 minutes. Serve immediately.

Tips for success: Beat mixture until fluffy. Pour batter immediately and quickly into heated muffin molds and slam into oven.

These are yummy plain or with jam, honey, etc. or even with the traditional gravy or sausage gravy or whatever you like on plain rolls. The rolls freeze well.

****

Here's a great recipe for fostering creativity, because it's amendable to amendments. I've never made a batch that wasn't very edible.

HUMMUS VERSION 1

1 can garbanzos (chick peas)
1 tablespoon olive oil
Salt and pepper to taste.

Drain can of garbanzos. Process all ingredients until smooth.
Eat.

This is the simplest version of hummus I know. It's tasty and versatile. You can use it as a spread or condiment on bread, crackers or chips. Or on rice. With a spoon. With your fingers. Or as a salad dressing. Or to make a broth soup rich and creamy, yum.

****

The more traditional version of
HUMMUS VERSION 2

1 can garbanzos
1 tablespoon tahini
1 clove garlic
1 tablespoon lime or lemon juice
pepper and salt to taste

Drain and rinse garbanzos. Process all ingredients until smooth. Eat. It's the tahini that gives the hummus its traditional flavor in this recipe.

Now for the creative fun: ENDLESS VARIATIONS WITH THIS FORGIVING BEAN SPREAD!

Here's a few additions to mix and match:

- Peanut butter (smooth, unsweetened) instead of the tahini or olive oil
- Real butter instead (very rich and creamy)
- 3 tablespoons nutritious yeast
- Add parsley, dried or fresh
- Add sesame seeds
- Add half a cup of chopped green onion before processing
- Add cumin
- Add sour cream (tart and creamy)
- Add Mexican seasoning
- Add Italian seasoning
- Add Curry spice
- Add Chinese Five Spice
- Use white beans instead of chick peas

****

Okay, I could go on. And on. And on. I can attest that all these variations are quite tasty. Be creative and try your own and you might be surprised at the delicious results!

- This recipe is easy and fun to make.
- This recipe saves time and money.
- This recipe is healthy and versatile.

Fruit Compote

1 can cherry pie filling
1 can pineapple chunks
2 apples (granny smiths work well)

Chop up apples into bite-size pieces. Mix all ingredients in a baking pan.
Heat in oven at 350 degrees.
Bake for 45 minutes.
Done.

Uses:

- Tasty alone.
- Yummy with ice cream, yogurt, sour cream, or whipped cream.
- Delicious on pancakes or waffles.
- Delightful on short bread or plain cake.

Variations are too numerous to list, here are a few. Again, be creative and think of your own!

- When baked, add walnuts, almonds or any nuts of your choice.
- Add raisins.
- Add cinnamon and/or nutmeg. Or cardamon. Vanilla works too.
- Use different fruits: blueberries, pears, apricots, etc. (no bananas.)

****

When we take good care of ourselves, we become more creative in every way. Here's a healthy breakfast that will keep you revved up and creating all morning.

HEALTH NUT WAFFLES

1/2 cup quick oatmeal
1/2 cup whole wheat flour
1/2 cup ground flaxseed (or increase amounts of oatmeal and flour)
2 tsp baking powder
2 tsp or more cinnamon
1 tsp vanilla
2 eggs
1/2 cup milk
3 tablespoons healthy oil

Mix dry ingredients together, then wet, let set for five minutes, add milk or egg if too dense to pour. Pour into waffle maker (should make about 4 good sized waffles) and cook. Eat and enjoy.

****

DEVILED EGGS CONDA STYLE

Take a dozen hard boiled eggs, cut in half, and remove the yolks. In a large bowl, place the yolks, a half cup of mayo (fat free works), a tablespoon or two of any mustard you like and... my secret ingredient, a tablespoon or two of curry spice. Blend well until smooth, and then spoon into the egg halves. Sprinkle with paprika or chili powder.

Eggs are healthy, and full of protein to keep you creating, so enjoy! Good brain food for being creative!

****

PUMPKIN NUT BREAD (I always buy big cans of pumpkin so I can make this)

1/2 cup sugar
1 ½ cup whole wheat flour
3/4 tsp cinnamon
1/2 tsp ginger
1 tsp nutmeg
1 tsp salt
dash cloves
1/2 cup vegetable oil
2 eggs beaten
1/3 cup water
1 cup cooked pumpkin (fresh or canned)
1/2 cup chopped pecans (or any nuts or can be omitted)
1/2 cup dark chocolate bits (can be omitted, but why?)

Grease 9x5x3 loaf pan (cake pan works too for a cake instead of bread, bake for a shorter period of time). Place all dry ingredients in large bowl, mix well. Add oil and eggs. Add water, pumpkin, nuts, and chocolate bits. Bake for 1 to 1 1/4 hours until done. Let cool and ease out of pan.

Variations:

- Use different spices, mace and allspice
- Use mashed sweet potato instead of pumpkin
- Frost if baked in cake pan with sprinkling chocolate bits on top and when slightly melted, spreading with a knife
- Frosting with cream cheese frosting works as well
- Add raisins or any dried fruits.

****

Another simple pumpkin recipe for the rest of the big can of pumpkin:

PUMPKIN CURRY SOUP
1 cup cooked pumpkin
1 cup milk, soy milk or broth of your choice
Curry powder to taste

Mix, heat and ENJOY!
Add any meat, including leftover Thanksgiving turkey, plus vegetables to make a hearty stew.

****

Whenever I give the following recipe to my English friends, they're puzzled by the name of these cookies. And snickerdoodles are different all over the country—here's my version:

SNICKERDOODLES
1 cup softened shortening of your choice (butter, margarine, Crisco)
1 1/2 cups white sugar
2 eggs
2 tsp cream of tartar
1 tsp baking soda
1/2 tsp salt
1 tsp nutmeg
2 3/4 cup white flour

Cream together the sugar and shortening then add the eggs and mix well, until somewhat fluffy. Mix the flour, cream of tartar, baking soda, nutmeg, and salt together and then add to the sugar, etc. Roll into walnut sized balls. Roll balls in mixture of 1/4 cup cinnamon and 1/4 cup sugar. Place unflattened onto ungreased cookie sheet and bake at 350 degrees 10-12 minutes until flat and *slightly* brown.

This makes a lot of chewy cookies, but that's never a problem.

****

Here's a great **BAKING POWDER BISCUIT** recipe:

2 cups white flour (can be unbleached)
1 tsp baking powder (I use more)
pinch of salt (omittable)
5-6 tablespoons of any oil or fat (I use canola)
2/3 cup of milk (soy ok)

Mix, dough will be stiff. Place on cookie sheet and bake. I usually don't bother to roll into roll shape, 'cause I like 'em weird, plunked on the cookie sheet, in free form sculptures that come out nice and crusty on the outside. But feel free to roll your dough into the more traditional shapes. 400 degrees for 15 minutes. Done.

You can use this recipe for dumplings or any recipe calling for expensive store bought roll dough.

See what you can make with a few ingredients? This is true in creating anything else, too.

****

MOLASSES CAKE
(This is one you can play with a lot, it is very forgiving.)

1/2 cup molasses (light or dark, your choice)
2/3 cup water
1/2 cup raisins (can be omitted, other dried fruits can be substituted)
1/2 tsp cinnamon
1/2 tsp cloves
1/2 tsp baking soda (I use more, about a teaspoon.)
1 and 3/4 cup white flour

Boil water, combine with molasses and raisins, boil 5 minutes (to soften dried fruit) let cool.

Combine other ingredients together, add mixture.

Spray 8" by 8" pan (or oil and flour) bake in 350 degree oven for 45 minutes.

I use more of the spices listed above and often add ginger and nutmeg, sometimes even a touch of chili powder. I often add a half cup of chocolate bits and/or a half cup of nuts. This cake is a little dry and not terribly sweet, so sometimes I melt chocolate bits on the top for a quick frosting. Sometimes I frost the cake, depending on mood. Plain, this makes a good breakfast cake.

****

This year, the **BASIL** in my garden exploded. So what to do with all the basil? Ah, and there's the link to increasing creativity, because after using it in spaghetti sauce and in tomato cucumber salad and giving it away to friends...what's next? I discovered that having such a wealth of one thing, basil, led me to be creative in how I thought about basil. It became much more than "one of the spices that goes into spaghetti." It expanded and took on a more complex role in my cooking in some unexpected ways.
Here are a few of the recipes I created:

- Preserve it. Rinse the basil, chop fine and bottle with olive oil. This can be used for the basil flavor alone or add garlic, onion, pepper, lemon, etc. and make salad dressing. Keep refrigerated when not using.
- Hang it upside down and dry it, although this is my least favorite way of preserving it. In my opinion, it loses a lot of flavor.
- My favorite is to rinse the leaves and put whole into a plastic bag and freeze. When the basil is frozen, crunch it up in the bag into little bits and use. It works great.

Now for a few recipes:

- Add basil to any curry to make it "Thai" style.
- Basil is great added to any Chinese dish, especially fried rice and chicken dishes.
- Add basil to ground chicken or any ground meat when making meatloaf.
- Puree basil with garlic and butter or margarine and spread on a halved French bread loaf, bake in oven (low temp or the basil will burn) for a twist on garlic bread.

****

My favorite way to use basil is a wonderful soup.

TOMATO BASIL SOUP
2 cups tomatoes (for spicier soup, can use 1 cup green tomatoes)
2 cups milk
1/2 cup basil (it will taste strong)
1 tablespoon olive oil
2 tablespoons nutritious yeast (optional)
Touch of pepper (optional)

Puree tomatoes. Heat olive oil in soup pan and add tomato puree and cook 5-8 minutes then add slowly the 2 cups of milk and simmer for 10 minutes, then add basil, yeast and pepper and simmer another 10 minutes. Soup will be thin. If you like thicker add 2 tablespoons of flour when adding milk and stir well.

****

When summer is done, green tomatoes abound. Because they contain all sorts of great anti-oxidants, tomatoes support all sorts of great brain activity. And what could be better than more brain activity, hence more creativity? So here's a couple of recipes:

HEALTHY GREEN FRIED TOMATOES
(Secret: They're healthy because they're not fried.)
There are two ways to make these, both are delicious.

For small green tomatoes, about a half pound. In a large bowl combine:
1/3 cup olive oil
1 tablespoon basil (fresh if you've grown it)
1 tsp garlic powder (or one fresh clove chopped very fine)
1 tsp onion powder (or tbsp chopped fresh, again very fine)
Pepper to taste if you like pepper

Chop small tomatoes into cubes, can be bite sized. Add to olive oil and spices and mix well. Pour into baking pan--works best if all pieces are touching but all on the bottom of the pan. Bake at 375 to 400 degrees (depending on your oven) for 10 minutes, then stir and bake for another 10 minutes or until still a little firm. Then sprinkle with Parmesan cheese if you like Parmesan cheese and broil until cheese is lightly browned.

For huge green tomatoes (beefsteaks for example):

- Make mixture.
- Place halved tomatoes in baking pan, best if touching.
- Drizzle 1/2 mixture over tomatoes.
- Bake for 15 minutes, then drizzle other half and bake for an additional 10-15 minutes until still slightly firm.
- Add Parmesan or broil plain to finish.

This simple recipe can be tweaked to your own personal tastes. For example, I can never use too much basil, especially if it's fresh. Use mozzarella cheese for a heartier dish or when you're ready to broil the tomatoes, add hot cooked ground beef and cheese for a main course. Simple, easy, healthy.

You can also toss green tomatoes into a soup or stir-fry. As long as they're cooked, they're delicious!

****

Here's another great recipe that's fast, simple, and tasty with easy variations and is full of anti-oxidants that are anti-carcinogenic and anti-aging. More brain food!

QUICK LOW FAT CURRY SOUP

2-3 cups chicken, beef or vegetable broth
Vegetables you like as much as you like
If you are a meat eater, add meat of your choice
Add curry spice by teaspoon to taste (caution: turmeric, the main ingredient in curry, has a bitter aftertaste if you use too much, so add slowly and taste often)

That's it. This is low calorie unless you use a high-fat meat (not recommended).

Additions that power up the anti-oxidant properties (add to your taste):

- Fresh garlic/onion
- Nutritious yeast
- Beans of any kind
- Olive or sesame seed oil (a tablespoon is plenty)

So eat up!

****

And finally, after you've been creating and working hard, here's an incredibly fast treat to reward yourself.

OOEY GOOEY CHOCOLATE MUG CAKE

4 tablespoons flour
4 tablespoons sugar
2-4 tablespoons cocoa
1 egg (or egg substitute)
3 tablespoons milk
3 tablespoons oil
3 at least tablespoons chocolate chips (I use a half cup and use dark chocolate.)
1 tsp vanilla
1 large, at least 16 ounce, mug or bowl (I use those big soup mugs.)

Place dry ingredients in mug and mix. Add egg and mix well. Then milk and oil and mix. Add the chocolate chips and vanilla and one last mix.

Place the mug in the microwave and nuke for 3 minutes on high. Don't worry if the mixture rises over edge of mug while cooking. Allow to cool before tipping out on plate (the chocolate chips sink to the bottom and provide a kind of icing).

Variations:

- Add rum or orange extract.
- Add any kind of nut.
- Top with whipped cream or sour cream or ice cream.

Can serve two, but can also be scarfed down by one!

****

Panocha

by Sheila Eismann

This is a recipe that my mother Rita used to make during every holiday season and has been passed down through the generations in our family. It has a sweet maple flavor mixed with walnuts and is truly par excellence!

Ingredients:

2 tablespoons butter or margarine
¾ cup half cream and half milk or rich top milk
1 cup brown sugar, firmly packed
1 ½ cups granulated sugar
1 tsp vanilla extract
¾ cup broken walnuts

Directions:

Melt butter or margarine in a medium sized (2 quart) saucepan with a heavy duty bottom, using a rubber spatula to bring it up and around the sides of the pan, greasing well.

Pour cream and milk into the pan. Place pan over medium heat and bring to a boiling point. Add brown and white sugars, stirring well to dissolve.

Cover pan and bring mixture to a boil slowly. Cook about 1 minute or until the sugar crystals are melted down from the sides of the pan.

Remove cover and continue gentle cooking without stirring to a soft ball stage (238 degrees F), about 20 minutes.

Remove from heat. Let stand without moving until candy is lukewarm (110 degrees F) and the bottom of the saucepan is barely warm to the hand. This will take about 1 hour.

Add vanilla and walnuts. Stir/beat with a heavy spoon until the candy becomes creamy and starts to lose its gloss.

Pour onto a plate, platter or into an 8 inch square. Cut into pieces while still warm. Enjoy!!

Meet the Authors

Suzanne Ames -After dropping out of school and graduating from the school of hard knocks, Suzanne earned her High School Diploma 32 years later and is currently pursuing her dream of writing. This is her first published work.

Sharon Brown is prone to flights of fancy and as such dreams of being a best-selling novelist or world-renowned Egyptologist or popular TV travel show host. She also dabbles at writing poetry and has enjoyed moderate success in this endeavor by having some of her poetry published. Her cowgirl poetry has been particularly well received. No one has been more surprised by this than she.

Married for over 20 years, **Terry Brown** and her husband Rock have 4 active teenagers. They have been in ministry all of their married life. Having grown up in a broken home, Terry has a passion for others to experience the healing love of God that she has come to know. She resides with her family in Meridian Idaho.

After years of working as a technical editor and writer, **Gina Burns** is now home watching her grandchildren and exploring new authoring possibilities. This is her first published work.

RoChel Burtenshaw finds her time occupied with her interior design business and her lovable one-year-old Shih Tzu named Sophia. Her two delightful daughters accuse her of spoiling the dog more than she ever did them as small children. RoChel just chuckles as she places Sophia's purple faux fur coat in the drawer and then tightens her little companion's hair bows.

An exercise instructor, **Conda Douglas** adores stretching in all forms. For more details, visit her blog, http://www.condasfitnesscenter.blogspot.com. Whenever Conda faces a writer's block, she bakes and it breaks! Visit her blog, http://condascreativecenter.blogspot.com for fun and creative hints, tips and secrets.

Of the five generations of female writers in her family**, Sheila Eismann** is blessed to represent the third one. She endeavors to be an encourager with a sense of humor as she pens her poetry and Bible studies for women.

Judy Ferro is a novelist and essayist who dabbles in poetry. Desiderata, the first book in her Karolus Chronicles, tells the story of a girl growing up as a hostage in the court of Charlemagne.

Fran Finkbeiner enjoys writing in all its forms. These days she's penning math proofs in her reach for a master's degree in mathematics. Her sexy, bald husband has been doing lots of cooking this semester for her and her three very independent teenagers.

Tina Frederick has been writing poems since she was ten years old and has had one recorded by a local heavy metal group. She has four children and five grandchildren and although she swore she would never go to church, Tina is active in her church.

Jane Freund is blessed and thrilled to be pursuing her lifelong passion for writing and publishing (she pinches herself each day but doesn't leave a mark)! Jane loves to laugh and to think, enjoys stimulating conversation and good books and is thankful for the many opportunities she has in her life. You can reach Jane at jane@janefreund.com.

Carol Garcia is an avid fan of life and new experiences which might explain her wide array of work experience which includes pineapple cannery canner, paralegal, college professor, technical trainer, tax preparer, tech buddy, and website developer and Internet marketer. Carol's inspiration to write came first from her college English professor - who had declared, "I should flunk you for missing so many classes, but your writing is too good" - then from her friends who were captivated by the stories of her travels.

Becky Grosenbach is a writer and speaker from Colorado. But mostly she's a wife and mother, trying to figure out how to get everything done from day to day. Becky attempts to live her life in a way that pleases God, believing that's what gives meaning to everything else.

Giselle Jeffries graduated from Boise State University with a major in English Writing and a minor in Spanish. She is presently a Realtor at Westerra Real Estate in Twin Falls, Idaho, but loves to write fiction and poetry during her free time.

Martha Kuhn is a frustrated writer turned school librarian. In her 80+ years of life, she has raised three children and has five grandchildren.

Angie Lewis has experienced a great deal of the United States, but after being born and raised in Idaho, has to say there is no place like home. She has always had a passion for writing, philosophy, and psychology and at this point in her life, she is thankful to be doing all three (two even greater loves: Rylea and Brad).

Suzanne McHone lives in Lewiston, Idaho and has been working on her degree in Creative Writing at Lewis Clark State College longer than she cares to admit. With children raised, grandchildren coming one after another, and a novel in the works, she has two semesters to go and is determined to finish before the great grandchildren show up.

Kathy McIntosh understands the power of a well-placed word. She is a professional book editor and speaker and writes humorous mystery fiction. She shares her insights on words, writing, and how to get your words read and appreciated at her blog, www.wellplacedwords.blogspot.com.

Buffy Naillon graduated Cum Laude from Boise State University with a degree in German Literature. She's been working in the media for over 10 years and counts among her professional credits "Der Spiegel" in Berlin, CBS Radio, "The Biggest Loser", and NPR News 91.

Benita Nelson lives in the Seattle area with her husband of...a long, long time. An avid consumer of mysteries and thrillers, she is a novelist who writes what she loves.

Jennifer Orvis was born and raised in Boise, Idaho. She loves creative writing of any kind and belly dancing. This is her first poem to be published.

Taffy Pullin writes under this pen name to candidly address the "sticky" issues of life to encourage and offer practical help to hurting women. Her faith, sense of humor, and perseverance are her most valuable survival tools. You can reach Taffy at taffy.pullin@gmail.com

Sheila Robertson explores the world in words and photographs. She lives and works in Boise, Idaho.

Lynette Sali, author, speaker, and artist from Boise, Idaho, is a blessed grandmother of six; she loves using wisdom gained in 40 years of marriage to encourage women. Contact her at lynette.sali@gmail.com.

Gena Shikles grew up in Idaho Falls, Idaho, where she said she would never date a sailor, never marry an engineer, never have only one child and never get out of Idaho!. Today she has been with the sailor she married 28 years ago who became an engineer, has one beautiful daughter, and lives in Singapore.

Janet Strong lives in Boise Idaho. I have written since I was young, but started seriously after 40 as a response to the life's ups and downs. I write for the glory of God and the encouragement of others.

Pamela Kleibrink Thompson is grateful for her family and the opportunity to contribute to the Pixie Chicks Anthology and to Jane Freund for starting the group. Pamela is a career coach, recruiter, and speaker. You can contact her at PamRecruit@q.com.

Jen Whitewing enjoys writing, being a mother, and a massage therapist. She has been married 15 years to her hero, Brian, who helps her with her writing.

Coming from Freundship Press in spring 2011

The Katrina Miracles
By Mel Surges

Writing Until I Get it Right – A Realist's Guide to Writing Professional-ly
By Jane Freund

For more details and to see other books of-fered by Freundship Press, visit www.freundshippress.com